Interdisciplinary Learning Activities

Interdisciplinary Learning Activities

Hannah Edelbroek

Myrte Mijnders

Ger Post

Amsterdam University Press

Volume 4 of the Series Perspectives on Interdisciplinarity

Cover design and lay-out: Matterhorn Amsterdam

Amsterdam University Press English-language titles are distributed in the US and Canada by the University of Chicago Press.

ISBN   978 94 6298 808 8
e-ISBN   978 90 4854 012 9 (pdf)
DOI   10.5117/9789462988088
NUR   143

Contents

1 Acknowledgements

The handbook *Interdisciplinary Learning Activities* is based on almost twenty years of experience with interdisciplinary teaching and learning. The materials and practices of the Institute of Interdisciplinary Studies at the University of Amsterdam contributed significantly to the framework of competencies and learning activities presented in this handbook. We are also grateful for the contributions from the bachelor programme Social Sciences at the University of Amsterdam and the US-based Association for Interdisciplinary Studies.

We would like to acknowledge the help provided by Noor Christoph, Linda de Greef, Christianne Vink, and Bregje Swart. Their suggestions, feedback and advice have been of great value. We would also like to acknowledge the valuable work provided by the editors of the previous edition: Tonja van Gorp, Mieke de Roo, Elke Stokker, Morten Strømme and Mirthe Hayes.

We are thankful for the support of all the other contributors who generously shared their experiences and provided us with useful information:

Shirley Berends, Sylvia Blad, Joris Buis, Tjard de Cock Buning, Karel van Dam, Steven Dijkstra, Jerome van Dongen, Esther van Duin, Merel van Goch, Andrea Haker, Anique Henderson, Miriam Janssen, Machiel Keestra, Wanda Konijn, Dominique Kunst, Frank Kupper, Marion van Lierop, Mieke Lopes Cardozo, Albine Moser, Fraser Nelson, Sietze Norder, Jessica Rodermans, Jaap Rothuizen, Lucas Rutting, Germaine Sanders, Jacintha Scheerder, Jasper ter Schegget, Joeri Scholtens, Hester Smeets, Vincent Tijms, Coyan Tromp, Iris van der Tuin, Matthijs Vlaar, Hylke de Vries, David Zetland and Cor Zonneveld.

2 Introduction

What would be the best way to have students acquire certain knowledge or learn specific skills? As a teacher you are faced with this question on a daily basis. What activity will motivate students to deepen their knowledge on a specific topic? How can students learn how to cooperate in groups? How can I promote integrative thinking?

These last questions have become more important in higher education, as the need for an interdisciplinary approach is increasingly felt. Professors and chancellors, for example, underscored the need to teach students how to integrate and apply their learning across multiple levels of schooling and across disparate fields of study (Association of American Colleges, 2007). The skills for integrative or interdisciplinary thinking tap into the 21st-century skills that have been identified as essential for a modern workforce dealing with demands of the knowledge economy (Voogt & Roblin, 2012).

Two main societal developments increasingly stress the need for teaching interdisciplinary skills. First, there is an expectation that scientists and professionals contribute to solving important societal issues. Second, the number of complex issues that are faced by society have increased because of technological advancements and globalization. Complex problems such as mental disorders, financial crises and climate change lie at the heart of interdisciplinary studies, as these problems cannot be comprehended from one disciplinary perspective alone. Climate change, for example, cannot be understood comprehensively 'without considering the influence of the oceans, rivers, sea ice, atmospheric constituents, solar radiation, transport processes, land use, land cover and other anthropogenic practices and feedback mechanisms that link this "system of subsystems" across scales of space and time' (National Academy of Sciences, 2004).

Does this need for interdisciplinary skills mean the end of teaching disciplinary knowledge and skills? On the contrary, we think that disciplinary and interdisciplinary approaches are complementary. In the disciplinary or reductionist approach laws and regularities become most apparent when scientists or experts in a field devote themselves to study a specific feature of a research object (Menken & Keestra, 2016). This information forms the basis for the interdisciplinary approach, where these disciplinary insights are integrated in order to come to a more comprehensive understanding of a complex problem (see for characteristics of a complex problem page 77).

Since the interdisciplinary approach is relatively young compared to the disciplinary approach, few practical resources are available that teachers in higher education can rely on. In a previous publication, authors of the Institute of Interdisciplinary Studies addressed several topics regarding designing interdisciplinary education, such as formulating and assessing interdisciplinary learning outcomes, embedding integration in the programme design, and didactic methods that nurture interdisciplinary understanding (De Greef, Post, Vink & Wenting, 2017). The current handbook builds on this work, in that it contains concrete suggestions in the form of examples of learning activities that you can use to teach and foster interdisciplinary skills in graduate and undergraduate students. The collection of interdisciplinary learning activities (ILAs) is not exhaustive. Our intention is to provide an initial series of inspiring learning activities that cover the most important aspects of interdisciplinary thinking. The ILAs in this handbook have been developed and tested by various teachers at different universities. We are confident that the incorporation of these ILAs into your courses will contribute to creating a successful, challenging and engaging learning environment.

Before we describe the different ILAs to enhance interdisciplinary thinking, we discuss in the next chapter what can be considered interdisciplinary understanding. Based on a literature review and the experiences of teachers and programme developers at the Institute of Interdisciplinary Studies, skills that constitute interdisciplinary understanding are discussed. The ILAs are then mapped onto these different skills (see the table on page 19).

3 Interdisciplinary understanding[1]

Interdisciplinary understanding consists of a set of interrelated constituent subskills, knowledge structures and attitudinal aspects that enable the synthesis of disciplinary insights and the construction of a more comprehensive perspective. Although there is much debate within the literature on the constituent skills of interdisciplinary understanding, we follow the categorization in the handbook by De Greef, Post, Vink and Wenting (2016). After reviewing the literature on interdisciplinary skills and an analysis with professors at the University of Amsterdam, they distinguished the following constituent skills for interdisciplinary understanding: critical thinking, collaboration and reflection. In this distinction, reflection is considered an essential supporting skill that is required for both critical thinking and collaboration (see the figure below).

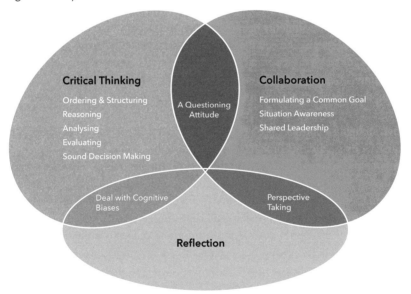

Skills and subskills that foster interdisciplinary understanding

Below these skills are described and further unravelled into constituent subskills.

---

1   This Chapter is adapted from work by Noor Christoph and Christianne Vink, which is described in paragraph 3.3 in the handbook Designing Interdisciplinary Education – a practical handbook for university teachers (De Greef, Post, Vink & Wenting, 2016)

Critical thinking

As stated in the introduction, in interdisciplinary education students should be able to think across the various disciplines that constitute their study programme or course. In order to connect and integrate these insights produced within different disciplines, students should be sensitive to the ways in which epistemological beliefs and assumptions vary between different disciplines. An analysis of differences and conflicts between disciplinary insights raises critical questions, such as 'how are concepts defined and measured in the disciplines?' and 'do disciplinary perspectives use the same concept yet mean something different?' (after Repko, 2008). Apart from evaluating these disciplinary insights, including identifying misinformation, disinformation, prejudice and one-sided 'monological' argumentation, critical thinking enables students to apply the integrated result to a particular context.

Facione (2011) comprises critical thinking into different subskills: **ordering and structuring, reasoning, analysing, evaluating and sound decision-making**.

In interdisciplinary projects, where students from different disciplines contribute, students can easily lose the overview. Skills to systematically collect, order and structure information are therefore important. **Ordering and structuring** information refers to appropriately discerning main points and side issues, and to reproducing and representing information in a logical and clear manner.

As interdisciplinary students need to analyse truth claims across disciplines, the ability to draw conclusions on the basis of arguments and to give due consideration to all relevant factors is essential in this work (Ivanitskaya et al., 2002; Nosich, 2012). **Reasoning** is the ability to underpin a statement with arguments or by using assumptions, draw inferences, refer to evidence and use these with clarity and precision.

When studying a complex problem such as climate change, a mental disorder or the financial crisis, students probably have to break the problem down into elementary components that can be studied (in the case of climate change: changes in solar inputs, ice-ocean coupling, human influences), while also analysing the interactions between these components (i.e. human influences on ice-ocean coupling). **Analysing** refers to conceptualizing a problem and capturing its essence in a short and concise way. It not only involves recognizing assumptions and examining the argument's logic to determine its validity, but also entails the systematic breakdown of a problem into meaningful smaller components, while being continuously aware of the intricate relationships between the components.

As with the other skills in critical thinking, **evaluation** is important in a disciplinary approach as well as the interdisciplinary approach. It entails weighing the evidence such as determining the validity of generalizations and conclusions from experimental data, distinguishing between weak and strong arguments, and recognizing fallacies and cognitive biases (Ivanitskaya et al., 2002; Terenzini & Pascarella, 1991).

After gathering all the disciplinary insights into a problem, **sound decision-making** enables students to choose a solution that integrates these insights and suits the specific context of the problem best. Sound decision-making is the skilful, responsible thinking that is conducive to good judgment because it is sensitive to context, relies on criteria and is self-correcting (Nosich, 2012). It entails the abilities to integrate information, use sound judgment, identify alternatives, select the best solution and evaluate consequences (Cannon-Bowers & Salas, 1997).

Collaboration

Collaboration relies heavily on communication. However, interdisciplinary or interpersonal communication is not easy, as implicit misunderstandings may arise concerning fundamental questions underlying the collaboration. What are valid data? What kind of results should emerge from the project (a publication, an intervention or perhaps software)? These assumptions can become explicit when students engage with each other in interdisciplinary teams (Menken & Keestra, 2016) and stress once more the importance of the critical-thinking skills described in the previous paragraph.

What is needed for a fruitful dialogue (and good collaboration) to occur between academics in different disciplines? First and foremost, students need to have an understanding of the theories, concepts and methodology that are central to their own discipline. But interdisciplinary communication asks more from students. Negotiating meaning, resolving differences, developing a shared understanding and communicating cognitive advancements to a broad audience is also important (Manathunga, Lant & Mellick, 2006).

Apart from strong communicative skills, interdisciplinary collaboration relies on the ability to work together in an efficient and goal-oriented way to achieve a product or outcome. Collaboration comprises different subskills such as **formulating a common goal, situation awareness and shared leadership**.

When students from different disciplines collaborate, they need to achieve consensus on a higher goal that exceeds individual, disciplinary stakes. **Formulating a common goal** often means that team members view their quest from broad horizons, exceeding their preferred professional discipline or worldview (Newell, 1990). **Situation awareness** requires being sensitive to the context of both the academic endeavour and team members' positions. During problem analysis, for example, it is important to be sensitive to implicit disciplinary implications of the wording of the problem and to be alert to whose interests are being advanced by choosing this problem over others (Newell, 2007).

Interdisciplinary team leadership is **shared leadership**: the leadership role may shift between team members in different stages of the process. This means that every team member should be capable to head a coherent team, value the unique contribution of each member and lead the team towards a successful result. Apart from skills to create a constructive environment, an interdisciplinary leader must be able to coordinate team and task processes (have project-management skills) and motivate team members, ensuring progression even when problem solving is difficult – which is common when addressing complex problems that are often ill-defined and multifaceted.

When crossing the borders of various disciplines, it is essential to have an open mind to deal with the problems that will arise. A **questioning attitude** is therefore required, where judgment is suspended and one is able to remain curious about the beliefs and motivations of the students from other disciplines. Having a curious, respectful and open attitude is important when working in an interdisciplinary context (Spelt et al., 2009; Paul & Elder, 2009), as it facilitates critical thinking and collaboration.

Reflection

Reflection plays an important role in any scientific process, as the aim of reflection is to understand why specific results have been achieved; how underlying assumptions, motives, and frameworks have (subconsciously) led to these results. Not only scientific content, but also individual and team performance can be reflected upon. Reflection is therefore seen as a supporting skill set for both critical thinking and collaboration.

Reflection comprises different subskills, of which **dealing with cognitive biases** and **perspective taking** are especially important in an interdisciplinary endeavour.

Everyone has cognitive biases in their knowledge, whether it comes from life experience or academic training. As we are often not conscious of how assumptions or beliefs affect our thinking, it is important to evaluate personal goals, priorities and values and to make them explicit. Only then can one **deal with cognitive biases**. This skill is especially important to improve integrative thinking since analysing assumptions and biases is often essential to find or create common ground between disciplinary perspectives.

Perspective taking – also referred to as role changing – is considered essential for interdisciplinary work. Repko, Szostak & Buchberger (2013), for example, list four reasons: Perspective taking (i) is necessary because of the complexity of the problem at hand (each perspective is by definition incomplete because it is embedded in a research paradigm); (ii) allows one to explore alternative viewpoints from different disciplines – thus exposing intersections where disciplines may be integrated; (iii) illuminates the general understanding of the problem and reduces tunnel vision – thereby reducing the possibility of important aspects being overlooked; and (iv) increases understanding of the significance of the disciplines involved and exposes the strengths and weaknesses of those disciplines.

With these definitions of the different interdisciplinary skills and their subskills in mind, we can map the ILAs onto these skills and subskills.

4 Interdisciplinary learning activities (ILAs)

Before we describe the 32 ILAs, some conditions and pointers are given to make the most out of these activities.

In this handbook we use the principle of constructive alignment, which is a form of outcome-based educational design connected to a constructivist understanding of learning (Biggs, 2011). Constructivists' view on learning is that students actively construct meaning and learn from what they are taught, integrating new material with previous knowledge and experiences (De Greef, Post, Vink & Wenting, 2017). In outcome-based course design a correct match between teaching aims, student learning outcomes and assessment criteria is pursued in order to make the overall learning experience transparent and meaningful to students (Biggs, 2003). Having a clear idea of what you want to achieve with your workshop, course or curriculum – and especially which aspects of interdisciplinarity you want to foster – is essential when deciding on learning activities.

In interdisciplinary learning, most of the learning outcomes are aimed at synthesis and evaluation, the highest tiers in Bloom's learning taxonomy. As described before, evaluation can be defined as weighing evidence, such as determining the validity of generalizations and conclusions, distinguishing between weak and strong arguments, and recognizing fallacies and cognitive biases. Synthesis comes closest to integration and can be defined as the ability of students to put together different parts (i.e. methods, theories and results across different fields and disciplines) and to create new patterns or structures, or propose alternative solutions or a more comprehensive result (De Greef, Post, Vink & Wenting, 2017). Many learning outcomes of the different interdisciplinary learning activities are aimed at synthesis and evaluation.

To implement an ILA in a successful way, there are a few important prerequisites (after De Greef, Vink, Post and Wenting, 2017). First, creating a safe learning environment is important for students to seek out perspectives they may find uncomfortable, to reflect on the limits of perspectives they hold and to find useful information in perspectives they may dislike. A safe learning environment invites students to be both critical and constructive towards the perspectives at hand. In order to create a safe environment, you can explicitly discuss how you and your students should collaborate and what values are important, make a habit of rewarding students for their efforts (and not only their results), and personally connect with students (see for more tips on how to create a safe learning environment De Greef et al., 2017).

Second, encouraging communication between students improves obtaining interdisciplinary learning goals such as learning to communicate and collaborate with students from various backgrounds. There are various techniques to encourage communication among students. For example, you can ask your students to prepare activities on topics of their discipline or expertise or stimulate class discussions with open-ended questions (see for more tips De Greef, Vink, Post & Wenting, 2017).

Third, make sufficient time for discussion and feedback, as these are valuable moments for evaluation and reflection. You can give feedback on how students communicate with each other in order to develop these skills – and the discussions subsequently. Last, in order to have students participate actively in the teaching activity, it may help to focus on their personal commitment. Motivation to actively participate is increased when students can connect the learning activity or the topic of their class to their personal goals. For example, you can ask at the start of the class what students already know about the topic. And ask them at the end of the class in what other situations they can apply their newly learned skills.

The ILAs have been categorized according to the length of the activity. We start with the learning activities that can be completed within one workshop. These are followed by activities that require several contact points during a course. Lastly, activities are outlined that are designed to be implemented in a curriculum, for example, because the student is asked to reflect on different courses or stages in the academic learning process.

The ILAs are described following the same format. First an overview (see example below) is provided to help you quickly scan the most important features of the learning activity, such as: what skills are trained with this activity, what its characteristics are (workshop, course or curriculum; individual or group activity), how long the activity takes, what the goal of the activity is, and what special requirements you need (under remarks). Second, the setup of the activity is outlined with a step-by-step walk through of the activity – from preparation to assessment. Third, examples are provided of what the activity may look like. Fourth, variations on the ILA are described. Lastly, references are listed.

Interdisciplinary skills	I.e. Reasoning, analysing, evaluating
Characteristics	■ Workshop, course or curriculum ■ Individual and/or group
Duration - activity	I.e. 90 minutes
Intended learning outcome	I.e. Students are able to compose an issue tree that adheres to the SEAL criteria
Remarks	I.e. In order to prepare for this workshop, the teacher has to read two papers from different disciplines on the problem

Table 1   Example of an overview listing the most important features of the learning activity

The following figure shows an overview of the ILA, mapped on the various skills and subskills that are trained in the activity. The numbers correspond to the skills that are trained most with the ILA, for example the ILA 'A Closer Look at Interdisciplinary Texts' mostly trains reasoning skills (1), and to a lesser extent skills in analysing (2) and evaluating (3).

Chapter	Workshop	Perspective taking	Formulating a common goal	Situation awareness	Shared leadership	A questioning attitude	Ordering & structuring	Reasoning	Analysing	Evaluating	Sound decision making	Deal with cognitive biases	Reflection
		Collaboration				Critical Thinking							
5	Issue Tree				3			1	2				
6	CALQ Discussion						3	2	1				
7	Breaking News	2							1				3
8	Business Model Canvas	3	2						1				
9	Socratic-Style Questioning					1					3	2	
10	Concept Map					2		1	3				
11	Elevator Pitch			3				1	2				
12	Interdisciplinary Debate	1							2	3			
13	Personal Strengths Matrix			3	2								1
14	Shuffling Teams			2		3				1			
15	Team Charters		3		2								1
16	Strengths Game	3			2								1
17	Walt Disney Strategy		2			1			3				
18	A Closer Look at Interdisciplinary Texts							1	2	3			
19	Complex Systems			3		1			2				
20	Designing a Research Question			2				3			1		
21	Finding a Shared Topic		2	1		3							
22	The Interdisciplinary Shuttle		1						2			3	
23	Managing Data					3	1		2				
24	Inter-professional Team Meeting		1		2								3
	Course												
25	Scenario Analysis			2					3		1		
26	Managing Teamwork in Big Groups		2	1									3
27	Developing a Campaign							3	2	1			
28	Stakeholder's View	2							1		3		
29	Movies & Matter		1					3	2				
30	Panel Discussion										3	2	1
31	OEPS Model					2					3		1
32	Developing a Collaborative E-book		3								1		2
33	Instrumental Sketchbook	2	1				3						
34	Writing a Reflection Essay			2		3							1
	Curriculum												
35	Reflection on (Inter)disciplinarity						2		3				1
36	Reflection on Different Perspectives	2							3				1

Workshops

5 Issue tree

Overview

Students learn a method to split up a complex problem into subproblems by drawing an issue tree. An issue tree easily illustrates all the important elements of a problem, and can help students to prioritize elements for their upcoming research process. There are two types of issue trees: diagnostic ones and solution ones. Diagnostic trees breakdown a 'why' key question, identifying all the possible root causes for the problem. A solution tree breaks down a 'how' key question, identifying all the possible alternatives to find a solution for the problem. This ILA is suitable for courses focusing on doing research in small groups, or as a starting point for an individual research paper or case study.

Interdisciplinary skills	Reasoning, analysing, shared leadership		
Characteristics	workshop	course	curriculum
	individual	group	
Duration – activity	90 minutes		
Intended learning outcome	Students are able to compose an issue tree that adheres to the SEAL criteria		
Remarks	Requirements: flip charts, markers		

Setup

a   Preparation teacher

Groups: make groups of 4-6 students, and make sure that all groups have a final version of their research question.

Individual: make sure that all students have a final version of their research question.

b   Preparation student

Students need to know the basic information about the topic they would like to research. They could either do the research individually or in a small group (4-6 persons). If you would like to do this ILA at the beginning of the course, you could give the students at least two papers to read before the first session. In addition, it is important that the research question for every group is already defined.

Teaching setup
Step 1

Explain why issue trees can help to structure and analyse complex problems.

1   You split up a complex problem into subproblems, which are easier to solve.
2   By doing this, the complexity of the problem decreases, since it will be easier to see which subproblems need to be solved in order to solve the main problem.
3   By drawing an issue tree with your group, you will create a common understanding of the main problem within a team, resulting in a shared vision.
4   The issue tree shows the missing elements for answering the main question or solving the main problem.

Step 2

Explain that it is essential that an issue tree is SEALed:

Similar: formulate every part in the same way. When you start with a 'how' question, your issue tree consists of layers related to that 'how' question.

Exhaustive: collectively exhaustive on every layer, cover everything. Make sure that your issue tree covers all relevant information per layer.

Apt: clear scheme, questions precise and focused. Make sure that everyone can follow your steps and understands the different layers.

Linear: no overlap, mutually exclusive. Concepts and words can only be in your issue tree once. If you see that two boxes consist of the same information, you should reorganize your layers.

See also the coloured boxes below and the example.

The format for an issue tree:

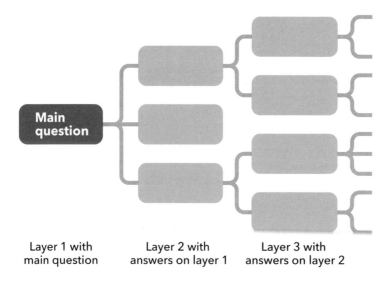

| Layer 1 with main question | Layer 2 with answers on layer 1 | Layer 3 with answers on layer 2 |

Step 3

Based on the type of questions the students are working with, there are two types of questions you can ask. If students are working on a question that diagnoses a problem, they can break the research question down with 'why 'questions. If they are working towards a solution of a problem, they can break the research question down with 'how' questions (see the example below: 'How can you increase excellence in primary education?').

Step 4

Explain how you start drawing an issue tree.
1   Start at the left with the main question;
2   The next layer, to the right consists of all questions necessary to answer the main question;
3   The next layer contains all questions necessary to answer the second column of questions, etc.

Example

Research question: how can you increase excellence in primary education?

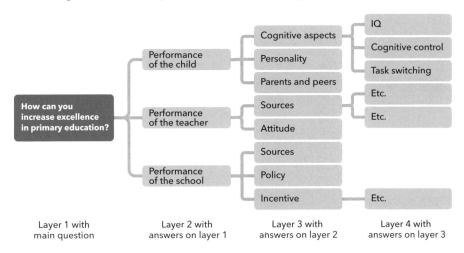

How is this issue tree made? The figure below helps you understand the building process.

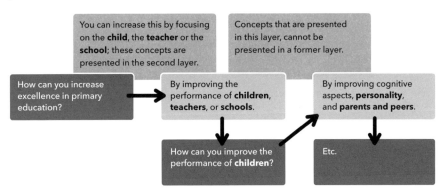

Variations

Students can also write down the main question and subquestions into the boxes of the issue tree (instead of the main concepts) if they think this is more insightful.

Tip: Be slow to share what you know as a teacher. If you come upon a group that is experiencing uncertainty or disagreement when filling in the issue tree, avoid the natural tendency to give the answers or resolve the disagreement. The learning that is accomplished through group work might be slower, but it is generally harder won and better for group performances.

References

The framework of this ILA is derived from the curricular design within the Institute for Interdisciplinary Studies, and was based on the issue tree method used at McKinsey & Company.

6 CALQ discussion

Overview

After a series of at least 10-12 lectures, students discuss and clarify the content of these lectures (including the literature) in groups of ten students. Each student prepares the discussion for one lecture via the CALQ format. This challenges students to look for the core of the lectures, to search for links and to explain to each other things that are unclear. This activity can help students to prepare for an exam.

Interdisciplinary skills	Analysing, reasoning and ordering and structuring		
Characteristics	workshop	course	curriculum
	individual	group	
Duration – activity	120 minutes		
Duration – homework	Each student should spend fifteen hours preparing for the discussion.		
Intended learning outcome	Students are able to summarize the core of the subject matter following the CALQ method; Students are able to chair a discussion about different disciplinary perspectives on a topic in interdisciplinary teams.		
Remarks			

Setup

a   Preparation teacher

Prepare a lecture series around a topic. Invite lecturers with different disciplinary backgrounds to explain their perspective on that topic. Ask the lecturers to include at least one scientific paper as study material. After the lectures, divide the students into groups of 10-12 students and assign at least one lecture to each student.

b   Preparation student

Each student studies one lecture from the lecture series plus the accompanying literature but also formulates the links with the other lectures and notes which things are unclear.

c   Teaching setup

Step 1

Explain to the students that next week at the CALQ Discussion they will discuss the entire lecture series including the literature in groups of 10-12 students. When everyone has presented his/her CALQ analysis, this means that students have discussed all the material for the exam.

Explain that during the discussion the students will chair the discussion on the lecture they prepared. Ask the students to make a CALQ analysis of the specific lecture and the accompanying literature as a whole. You can also decide to allocate one article to every student. This CALQ analysis will help shape the discussion. To be able to discuss all of the topics, each student should read and study not only the topic that has been assigned to him/her, but also the other lectures and articles.

Tip: To stimulate students to not only study the lecture they prepare a CALQ for, but the other lectures as well, you can have the students formulate at least one link with every other lecture.

A **CALQ** consists of:

Core message:	Write down the lecturer's core message from the lecture/literature in a sentence/couple of sentences that comes closest.
Argument:	Summarize the lecturer's point of view on the central topic. Try not to repeat the PowerPoint slides, but rather try to explain the lecturer's line of reasoning: how did he/she construct the evidence that led to his/her conclusion?
Link:	Indicate how this topic relates to other subjects during this course.
Question:	Prepare three questions or statements about this topic that you believe might be good questions for the exam. One of the questions needs to be aimed at a topic that is unclear to you (or that you expect to be unclear to others).

Step 2

At the workshop (a week after the explanation of the activity) every student acts as chairperson for ten minutes for the specific lecture they prepared. In these ten minutes, they present their CALQ-analysis. It is the chairperson's responsibility to ensure that 1) everybody pays attention and takes part in the discussion; 2) all relevant issues get discussed; and 3) this all happens in ten minutes. Note that the final questions or statements are an important element of the CALQ analysis.

To create a fruitful discussion, it is essential that the students not only present their CALQs but also ask well-aimed questions to their peers so that they get a conversation going with input from students with other disciplinary backgrounds to get a better understanding of the study material.

Tip: Plan enough time for students to reflect on their peers and provide a supportive environment in the classroom encouraging the re-evaluation of conclusions, to ensure that the students do not blindly trust what their fellow students present as their CALQ, but critically reflect upon their peers' input.

d   Assessment

You could grade the chairing of the CALQ discussion on content.

Content			
Bad	**Poor**	**Sufficient**	**Good**
The chair meets none of the six criteria:	The chair meets two of the six criteria:	The chair meets four of the six criteria:	The chair meets all of the following criteria:
1 is well prepared;	1 is well prepared;	1. is well prepared;	1 is well prepared;
2 introduces goal of the discussion;	2 introduces goal of the discussion;	2 introduces goal of the discussion;	2 introduces goal of the discussion;
3 keeps the discussion focused on the topic;	3 keeps the discussion focused on the topic;	3 keeps the discussion focused on the topic;	3 keeps the discussion focused on the topic;
4 summarizes regularly the content of the discussion;	4 summarizes regularly the content of the discussion;	4 summarizes regularly the content of the discussion;	4 summarizes regularly the content of the discussion;
5 asks peers to clarify explanations;	5 asks peers to clarify explanations;	5 asks peers to clarify explanations;	5 asks peers to clarify explanations;
6 encourages participants to deepen their knowledge of the subject.	6 encourages participants to deepen their knowledge of the subject.	6 encourages participants to deepen their knowledge of the subject.	6 encourages participants to deepen their knowledge of the subject.

Example

In the course Water Governance students prepare the exam with a CALQ discussion. For example, a student made this CALQ of the lecture '*The Challenges for the Twenty-First Century: A Critical Approach*' based on an article by Gupta & Dellapenna (2009).

1   Core message: What is the most important message that the author tries to bring across?

'The history of water law is the history of the struggle to control water and to manage the pollution associated with water. The struggle is manifest in rules of ownership and access, and whether power should be centralized or decentralized' (Gupta & Dellapenna, 2009, p. 408).

2   Argumentation: Try to explain the line of argumentation.

Water law

In the 21st century water is increasingly considered an economic good following neoliberal thinking. However, it is more complex. Four factors have influenced the variation in water law across time and space: Water geography, Economic dependence, History and Hydro-politics. Differences in water law are present, but there are eight forces that explain the overall global convergence of water law: 1) civilizations spread initial rules; 2) religious development; 3) conquest and colonization (spread rules to different places in the world); 4) communist ideas (water state controlled and nationalized); 5) legal codification (in the nineteenth and twentieth centuries more systematic and more effective); 6) rise of epistemic and engineering communities (new literature on water); 7) rise of environmentalism (pollution and impact biodiversity important and sustainable development); and 8) rise of private sector engagement.

Global Trends

The history of water law is one of ever-changing norms, rules and practices, with considerable differences between the global north and south. In the south there are more pluralist and fragmented water laws while in the north the water laws show more coherence. The overlapping systems in the south are mostly a result from colonial histories experienced by these countries. This lead to disharmony due to different policies about a river basin in the same state and disharmony due to pressure created by diverging actors. Therefore, water law is not constant. Furthermore, there are a lot of changes in the notion of ownership and changes in centralization vs decentralization. Now a lot of decentralisation of private or public participation is present.

To manage the water law principles as a baseline in international water law do exist. However, the challenges for these principles are to be translated into concrete arrangements. Another way of management is the harmonization of global trends to promote common approaches, but they can be conflicting with local cultural approaches or indigenous law. There is no linearity in history.

Challenges

Access to drinking water and sanitation is needed for poverty alleviation. However, water is increasingly commodified following the economic logic of managing scarce resources. Additionally, along with water access, water depletion, water pollution and climate change are profound emerging challenges. A solution can be that the law needs to be open to other disciplines to solve complex matter about water. Additionally, there should be an integrated assessment panel on water issues such as the IPCC exists for climate change. Moreover, fairness and equity issues should be better implemented based on principles laid down in global treaties.

Conclusion: At different levels on water law there are a lot of changes. These changes show that water law is very complex and that water governance needs to be improved across the globe.

3   Link: Indicate how the lecture and literature relate to the other literature (overlap and/or complementary?).
    This article shows the history of water law and can be seen as the baseline for the other articles. Moreover, the challenges of water governance are explained in the other articles of Gupta, but also in the articles about water grabbing the challenges of water governance are present. For instance, economic need is often a driver in water grabbing. Additionally, the history of water law is put forward as being very dynamic and it could be important to understand this when studying several water grabbing cases.

4   Questions: Match the right numbers with the right letters of the table below, and provide an argument why these concepts match.

1 fragmented water laws	a from principles to concrete arrangements
2 international water law	b sustainable development
3 rise of environmentalism	c postcolonial societies
4 multiple coexisting legal systems	d legal pluralism

(answers)

1-c   In the south, water laws are often fragmented as a result from colonial histories;

2-a   International water laws consist of principles, but these principles need to be translated into concrete arrangements to change something;

3-b   The rise of environmentalism includes the recognition of the term Sustainable Development;

4-d   Situations of legal pluralism are often encountered in waterscapes, and imply that multiple legal norms apply simultaneously to the same situation.

Variations

Apart from grading on content, you can also grade the student who chairs the CALQ discussion on group dynamics. By only grading the chairing of the discussion you allow students to share their uncertainties about their CALQ analysis and this may improve the quality of the discussion.

You can also grade students on both content and group dynamics. However, this may be too much to handle for most students and should be kept for highly motivated and excellent students.

Groups Dynamics			
The chair meets less than two of the following criteria: 1 lets every peer participate; 2 stimulates the conversation between peers; 3 inhibits excessive speakers; 4 listens to all the contributions.	The chair meets two of the following criteria: 1 lets every peer participate; 2 stimulates the conversation between peers; 3 inhibits excessive speakers; 4 listens to all the contributions.	The chair meets three of the following criteria: 1 lets every peer participate; 2 stimulates the conversation between peers; 3 inhibits excessive speakers; 4 listens to all the contributions.	The chair meets all of the following criteria: 1 lets every peer participate; 2 stimulates the conversation between peers; 3 inhibits excessive speakers; 4 listens to all the contributions.

References

The framework of this ILA is derived from the programme Future Planet Studies curricular design within the Institute for Interdisciplinary Studies.
The grading of the chairman role is partly based on Bonset, H. & Braaksma, M. (2008). *Het schoolvak Nederlands onderzocht*. Utrecht: SLO, Nationaal Expertisecentrum Leerplan Ontwikkeling.

7 Breaking news

Overview

Students are presented with a specific 'worldview' or theory presented in an academic paper they've read in preparation for class. During the workshop a new theory is presented: the breaking news. In group discussions students explore the contrast between these theories and whether they can be synthesized.

Interdisciplinary skills	Analysing, perspective taking, reflection		
Characteristics	workshop	course	curriculum
	individual	group	
Duration - activity	45-90 minutes		
Intended learning outcome	Students are able to detect the assumptions underlying a theory; Students are able to describe the implications of a theory; Students are able to describe how the assumptions underlying different theories can prevent integration of these theories.		
Remarks			

Setup

a   Preparation teacher

Optional: preparing a lecture on the basic principles of a knowledge framework (see setup step 1).

b   Preparation student

Preparation student

Optional: Reading an academic article (see setup step 1).

Teaching setup
     Step 1
     Have students read an article in which a specific knowledge framework or worldview
     is explained. You can also choose to give a short lecture on a worldview, however, take
     into account that this will add an extra 15-20 minutes to the learning activity.

     Step 2
     After reading the article or listening to the lecture, the students detect the main
     assumptions and implications of this worldview by, for example, answering the
     following questions (after Paul & Elder, 2014):
     - What are the key concepts?
     - What are the main conclusions of this theory?
     - What assumptions have led to these conclusions?
     - What is taken for granted in the theory?
     - What are the implications of this theory?
     (Also see The Socratic method on page 41)

     Step 3
     Start the (second part of the) lecture with a presentation of the 'breaking news', for
     example, by means of a video clip or an article. This breaking news is in contrast
     with the previous worldview. Have the students detect the main assumptions and
     implications of this worldview again.

     Step 4
     Start a group discussion on the differences between the worldviews. As a teacher, you
     could facilitate the discussion by focusing on the following questions:
     1   How does this breaking news complement/contrast with the previous worldview?
     2   Which assumptions within the first worldview have to be reconsidered?
     3   Is it possible to incorporate the implications of the breaking news into the
         worldview (i.e. by changing current assumptions or by adding new assumptions
         to the knowledge framework)?

     It is also possible to confront the students with the three questions separately; this
     will allow the moderator to structure the discussion more easily.

Example

Human Behaviour: The Impact of Nature vs. Nurture
Start the lecture by presenting the following worldview to the students. This is the
framework they start the learning activity with (step 1 and 2):

Step 1 and 2: Karl Marx's worldview
Karl Marx (1818-1883) was a philosopher, an economist, a historian and a journalist,
but is best remembered as a revolutionary socialist. He believed that the nature of
human beings was largely determined by the political and economic characteristics
of the social system that was prominent during his time. He is perhaps best known

for his perspective on how economic power relations resulted in a ruling class of capitalists who owned all productive property, and an oppressed class of labourers who could not do much more than sell their labour. His revolutionary ideas on how the labouring classes would eventually liberate themselves from their social position is an illustration of his belief that individuals could evolve in a different way if a specific social system were abolished, thus reinforcing the belief that human behaviour is a product of the circumstances and past experiences (i.e. nurture) of the individual.

Step 3: Charles Darwin: breaking news

Charles Darwin (1809-1882) was educated in the tradition of natural theology, a philosophy that tried to unite religious ideas with scientific discoveries, but his discovery regarding the origin of species would largely affect the assumptions of this knowledge framework and that of others (like that of Marx). Darwin discovered that the evolution of species is driven by natural selection and that our common struggle for survival is largely genetically programmed. This discovery highlighted the controversial idea that human beings evolved from animals and that all organisms are the product of environmental pressures and subsequent (random) adaptations. This discovery also placed a big question mark over the extent to which human beings have a free will and/or consciously perform their actions.

Step 4: Background information for the lecturer to help the student during the group discussion: Reconsidering the old worldview

An implication of Darwin's theory for the given worldview was the belief that the talents and dispositions of individuals are primarily determined not by class and/or social structures but by our biological characteristics. By incorporating the breaking news into the worldview of Marx, students may come up with reconsiderations that relate to the field of sociobiology (of which Edward O. Wilson was the father), which studies the biological mechanisms behind human behaviour that emerged from Darwin's discoveries as an initially controversial discipline.

Darwin's discoveries had obvious implications for the natural sciences but also served to redefine the social sciences. Whereas beforehand social science was perceived as an individual academic discipline – since the assumption was that the behaviour of humans is fundamentally different from animals and therefore cannot be studied in the same way – this distinction was no longer so clear-cut.

An implication of the breaking news for the worldview presented by Marx could be to challenge the extent to which the individual lives of people could be altered by changes within the social system, as it now appears that certain dispositions are biologically (as opposed to socially) determined. Whether this new insight increases or reduces the potential of the revolutionary socialist ideas of Marx, could be an interesting point of discussion.

Drug addiction: biological addiction versus psychological and social factors

Proof of chemical addiction came in the 1960s from experiments on rats, mice, monkeys and other captive mammals. In these experiments animals were put in isolated cages, connected to a self-injection apparatus, and taught to self-administer drugs by pressing a lever in the cage. By the end of the 1970s hundreds of experiments of this sort showed that animals choose drug injections in preference to food and water, and that these animals would sometimes even kill themselves slowly (Woods, 1978). According to some researchers, these results show that the power of these drugs to instill a need for future consumption 'transcends species and culture and is simply a basic fact of mammalian existence' (Alexander, 2001). As one researcher put it: 'If a monkey is provided with a lever, which he can press to self-inject heroin, he establishes a regular pattern of heroin use – a true addiction – that takes priority over the normal activities of his life... Since this behaviour is seen in several other animal species (primarily rats), I have to infer that if heroin were easily available to everyone, and if there were no social pressure of any kind to discourage heroin use, a very large number of people would become heroin addicts' (Goldstein, 1979).

The idea that someone is instantly addicted to a drug like heroin or cocaine, and once he or she is addicted is powerless against the drug, is in accordance to the narratives in many drug users' reports. These addicts describe how using the drugs instilled an irresistible drug appetite and destroyed an otherwise happy life (Burroughs, 1959; Courtwright, Joseph & DesJarlais, 1989; Lemere & Smith, 1990; Waldorf, Reinarman & Murphy, 1991).

Researchers at Simon Fraser University had reservations about the chemical addiction research cited above. They especially wondered whether the conditions these animals found themselves in (the isolated cages) contributed to the addictive behaviour. These researchers wondered whether social creatures like rats would also develop an addiction in conditions that were more 'natural'? In order to test their idea, they built an airy and spacious (about 200 times the square footage of a standard laboratory cage), scenic, comfortable (with toys on the floor) and sociable (with 16-20 rats of both sexes in residence at once) environment. The rats living in Rat Park, as it came to be called, had 'little appetite for morphine' (Alexander, 1985); under some conditions they consumed twenty times less morphine than the rats in the cages. From these experiments it was concluded that chemical addiction was not the strongest factor influencing the rats' habits. The rats' drug taking varied with physical, mental and social setting, rather than becoming identically spellbound by addiction.

Although media coverage sometimes describes drugs like crack cocaine as 'the most addictive drugs on earth' and causing 'instant addiction', these claims are simply false (Alexander, 2001). 'The great majority of users of crack and other forms of smokable cocaine are experimenters who smoke cocaine a few times and subsequently lose interest. There are also a number of users who use it intermittently over longer periods without serious difficulty.' Davies (1992) argued that addicts attribute causes to their own behaviour mainly to the drug for the purpose of maximizing their self-esteem, rather than describing reality. 'To claim that one has been transformed into an addict by exposure to a drug can serve the same function as pleading guilty to a lesser offence: Rather than bearing responsibility for unacceptable behaviour, the person is only responsible for the unwise experimentation that transformed him or her into an addict, against their best intentions' (Alexander, 2001).

Step 4: Background information for the lecturer to help the student during the group discussion: Reconsidering the old worldview

The first worldview has many implications for the treatment of drug users. What is the role of the addict in dealing with the addiction? And what professional(s) could help a drug user following this worldview? Would someone be helped with a psychologist, social worker, or psychiatrist? And what professional(s) is/are needed to treat an addict after the breaking news?

Despite the empirical evidence, the conventional belief in chemical addiction persists, because, as Alexander (2001) argues, it serves personal, political and commercial needs. The personal needs of addiction users have been discussed above. How does the chemical addiction serve the other needs? For example, one can argue that the frightening idea of a powerful drug has served political agendas in securing funds for the war on drugs. Alexander (2001) also detects an important commercial reason why drug companies support the belief in chemical addiction: heroin and cocaine can be produced cheaply and are therefore a potential threat to the drugs that produce substantial profits for the drug companies. 'There is no pharmacological reason that heroin and cocaine are prohibited for virtually all purposes, whereas drugs which share all the same positive effects as well as addictive qualities – for example, meperidine (tradename: Demerol) and methylphenidate (tradename: Ritalin) – are legally prescribed.'

Variations

You may decide to have a group of students act as the (neutral) moderator during the discussion.

Depending on the overall purpose of the course in which this method is applied, the breaking news may be invented or real. For example, referring to a real discovery within a specific research discipline that fundamentally changed previous assumptions within that field (e.g. the relative influence of epigenetics in biology) may be relevant, in particular to acquaint the students with former beliefs within a specific research discipline.

Request that if students challenge others' ideas, they back it up with evidence, appropriate experiences, and/or appropriate logic. If the group starts to veer in the direction of negativity and/or pointless venting, ask them how they would like to address this and step back when a group is functioning.

Let students reflect on their role in the group discussion. They may do so either orally or in writing. This reflection helps them to discover how they functioned in the group.

References

The framework of this ILA is derived from the curricular design within the Institute for Interdisciplinary Studies.

- Alexander, B.K. (2001). The Myth of Drug-Induced Addiction. A paper delivered to the Canadian Senate. Retrieved from http://www.canadianharm-reduction.com/sites/default/files/The%20myth%20of%20drug%20 induced%20addiction.pdf
- Alexander, B.K. (1985). Drug use, dependence, and addiction at a British Columbia university: Good news and bad news. *Canadian Journal of Higher Education*, 15, 77-91.
- Davies, J.B. (1992). *The myth of addiction: An application of the psychological theory of attribution to illicit drug use.* Switzerland: Harwood Academic Publishers.
- Buskes, C. (2009). *Evolutionair Denken: de Invloed van Darwin op ons Wereldbeeld*, Editorial: Nieuwezijds: Amsterdam.
- Goldstein, A. (1979). Heroin maintenance: A medical view. A conversation between a physician and a politician. *Journal of Drug Issues*, 9, 341-347.
- Woods, J.H. (1978). Behavioral pharmacology of drug self-administration. In M.A. Lipton, A. DiMascio, and K.F. Killam (Eds.), *Psychopharmcology: A generation of progress.* New York: Raven.

8 Business model canvas

Overview

This ILA connects science to business and society and can be used when small teams of students carry out research and provide consultancy on an issue identified by the project client and produce clear, practical recommendations. Drawing a Business Model Canvas helps students to make a quick-scan analysis of an organization by systematically focusing on several business elements, and therefore obtain an overall view of all the important elements of the organization.

Interdisciplinary skills	Analysing, formulating a common goal, perspective taking		
Characteristics	workshop	course	curriculum
	individual	group	
Duration – activity	90 minutes		
Intended learning outcome	Students are able to perform a business model canvas analysis[2] of an organization.		
Remarks	Scheme from www.businessmodelhub.com Post-its		

Setup

a Preparation teacher

Find a company/organization that connects to the aim of the course or the specific topic of your workshop. Fill in the business model canvas for yourself. This could function as an example to explain the aim and elements of the business model canvas to the students.

---

2 See business model canvas from www.businessmodelhub.com

b   Preparation student

If you want students to fill in a business model canvas for a company/organization of their own choice, let them bring information of that company/organization to class.

c   Teaching setup

Step 1

At the start of the course, divide the students into groups of around four students. Every group chooses its own leader. This leader acts as the moderator.

Step 2

Start the tutorial by explaining the business model canvas using a blank canvas. Make sure that you cover the different elements of the canvas. For example, how is it used in practice? And: what is the aim of filling in the canvas? You can explain that the left part of the canvas covers internal organizational aspects, and the right part focuses on customers. Furthermore, the canvas can help you (and organizations) to see all the important elements of an organization and visualize the connections between them.

In addition, give an example of a filled-in canvas and explain these questions based on the filled-in canvas (see examples).

Key Partners	Key Activities	Value Propositions	Customer Relationships	Customer Segments
	Key Resources		Channels	
Cost structure			Revenue streams	

Step 3

Every group receives the business model on A3-sized paper. Students can either choose a company, develop a company or have one assigned to them by the lecturer. Instruct the groups to fill in the business model canvas. Ask the students to start with the customer segment and write down the company's clients on Post-its. Explain that every customer has her/his own colour post-it. These colours are used when an activity or a definition relates to a customer in the rest of the model. The model is completed when all customers are known, and all the elements of the model are filled in.

Step 4

After the entire business model is completed, the students analyse the strong and weak points of the organization. Ask the students to assign a + for strong points, or a − for weak points to every Post-it.

Next, the students think about how the organization could be improved. Let the students formulate solutions to the weak points.

End the session with presentations of all the groups, in which they share their insights.

Tip: Ask a student from the previous class/ year to assist you with this activity. Having participated in the struggles first-hand in the previous year, the student co-teacher brings an invaluable voice of experience to the new group.

Tip: Invite the project client to the presentation session.

Example

Your course focuses on the development of a project for locals in a poor neighbourhood. As an example you will give your students a business model canvas of an organization, which uses a piece of land where they can educate the (unemployed) locals about agriculture. These locals could then produce vegetables and sell them to the people in their neighbourhood. The vegetables are low-priced because of the poverty in this area. The common goal is to produce local-made, cheap and healthy food.

Key Partners	Key Activities	Value Propositions	Customer Relationships	Customer Segments
The local primary school +	Education of the volunteers –	Delivery of cheap, healthy, local-grown vegetables +	Local community +	Poor locals +
The local community centre +	Production +			People who eat unhealthy food -
The local government –	**Key Resources**		**Channels**	
	Volunteers +		The local primary school +	
	A large piece of land –		The community centre +	
	Tools for agriculture –		Word of mouth +	
	Seeds +		Social media +	

Cost structure		Revenue streams	
Production -		A bag with vegetables +	

Variations

Add the disciplines or backgrounds of the customers to the Post-its in order to gain insight into the different interests.

References

Alexander Osterwalder and Yves Pigneur, www.businessmodelhub.com

9 Socratic-style questioning

Overview

Socratic-style questioning is an important tool to train a questioning attitude (and therefore critical thinking). This method trains students to ask questions that help them to gain insight into underlying assumptions and values of (disciplinary) perspectives. By asking Socratic-style questions students have an opportunity to reflect on their own perspective and detect their cognitive biases.

Interdisciplinary skills	A questioning attitude, reflection, dealing with cognitive biases		
Characteristics	workshop	course	curriculum
	individual	group	
Duration – activity	90 minutes		
Intended learning outcome	Students are able to use the Socratic-style questions to detect underlying assumptions and values of a perspective on a complex problem.		
Remarks			

Setup

a   Preparation teacher

Book a classroom where the tables and chairs can be easily moved around so you can sit down in a circle and the participants can see each other. As a teacher you should join the circle.

Tip: Make sure you know the names of the students.

b   Preparation student

The students prepare by making an overview of their disciplinary perspective on the complex issue that will be discussed in the workshop. For example, they make a short summary of different research articles.

c   Teaching setup
        Step 1
        Explain that the goals of this exercise are to detect underlying assumptions and
        values of different disciplinary insights, and to find out what lies at the root of the
        conflict between these insights. During this exercise, students use the method of a
        Socratic dialogue. The goal of a Socratic dialogue is to make underlying assumptions
        of someone's perspective explicit. The aim is not to find a solution.
        In addition, explain the important rules of a Socratic dialogue to the students:
        1   Respect the participants;
        2   participate in the conversation;
        3   ask open and meaningful questions;
        4   listen to each other by summarizing what you heard and use probing questions;
        5   allow for silences to digest the information.

        Tip: Ask the students what they think is needed for an effective dialogue and try to
        incorporate their ideas in the dialogue.

        Step 2
        After the instruction of the exercise, divide the students into small teams of five
        students. These teams could be related to their research project, but could also be
        random for this exercise. Instruct the teams to determine which disciplinary insights
        conflict each other. Invite the students to ask each other clarification questions
        about these conflicting insights. Ask the groups to write down the underlying
        assumptions they discovered. You could give students a hand-out with the suggestion
        for questions they could ask. Walk around to monitor if students use the Socratic
        method. You could also steer the direction of the dialogue by summarizing often and
        allowing silences.

Example

        You can use these questions to encourage students 1) to talk about and share ideas
        with each other, and 2) to question the implications and consequences of what they
        are saying.

        Examples of questions
        Questions for clarification:
        ■ Could you explain this?
        ■ If you were to rephrase this, what would you say?
        ■ What do you think is the main issue here?

        Questions to check assumptions:
        ■ What are the assumptions when stating this idea?
        ■ How could you falsify or verify this assumption?
        ■ What alternative assumptions do you see?
        ■ All your reasoning depends on the idea that... Can you explain why you choose...
          rather than...?

Questions for reasons and proof:
- What could be a reason to question this proof?
- Can you explain why you think... follows from...?
- What led you to believe this...?
- What would you say to someone who said...?

Questions to explore alternative perspectives:
- How could this be viewed differently?
- What are the strengths and weaknesses of this approach?
- Would there be other disciplines that could shed light on our topic?

Questions for implications and consequences:
- What would happen if...?
- What are you implying by this?
- If this and this is the case, what else must be true?

Questions to question the question:
- What is the goal of this question?
- Can we break down the question?
- To answer the question, what other questions must we target first?

Variations

This ILA can be part of an interdisciplinary research project.

You could add an extra step by letting the students present the assumptions they discovered.

You could let the students rank the assumptions by importance.

The outcomes of this Socratic dialogue could be the starting point to create common ground between disciplines by using integration techniques. For example, you could incorporate this activity with 'Managing Data' (see pag 95).

References

The framework of this ILA is derived from the curricular design within the Institute for Interdisciplinary Studies.

De Greef, L., Post, G., Vink, C., Wenting, L. (2017). *Designing Interdisciplinary Education: a practical handbook for university teachers*. Amsterdam, Amsterdam University Press.

10 Concept map

Overview

In a concept map students (visually) represent their knowledge regarding a (complex) topic. In making a concept map students train their analytical skills, as they have to draw links between key concepts and related ideas, and they have to show the hierarchy between the different levels of concepts/ideas. This ILA could also be used at the start of a research project, when students have to narrow down a (complex) issue in order to make it feasible to study.

Interdisciplinary skills	Reasoning, a questioning attitude, analysing		
Characteristics	workshop	course	curriculum
	individual	group	
Duration – activity	60 minutes		
Intended learning outcome	Students are able to draw up a concept map to visualise the type of relations (cause-effect, correlation), between several concepts and themes.		
Remarks	Blank sheets of paper or flip charts		

Setup

a   Preparation teacher

Prepare a presentation including the main goals of a concept map and an example of a concept map connected to your course.

b   Teaching setup

Step 1

Start the lecture with an introduction on the concept map. Explain the main goals: to explore a research topic with an open mind, and to visualize relations between several concepts and themes within that topic. In addition, show one example of a concept map to the students.

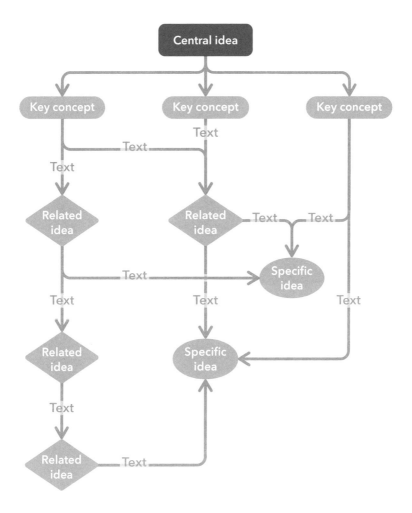

Derived from www.lucidchart.com/pages/concept-map

Step 2

Divide the students into small groups of around four students. If students have to do a research assignment in another course, let them work in these groups. If not, let them form groups of approximately four and have them choose a topic in no more than ten minutes.

Step 3

Have students draw their concept map on A4-sized sheets or flip charts. They can surf the internet to find information to fill gaps or to find information on the relations between concepts. Note that they not only have to focus on individual concepts, but also on the type of relations (cause-effect, correlation) between concepts. Instruct students to label the relationships between the concepts, and to think carefully about these words.

c   Assessment

If you would like to provide feedback on a concept map, you could check the following aspects:

- Are the relations between the concepts clearly presented and correct?
- Is the concept map complete?
- Does it make sense that concepts are related to each other?

Example

A teacher in cognitive neuroscience used the following concept map to explain the structure of a concept map.

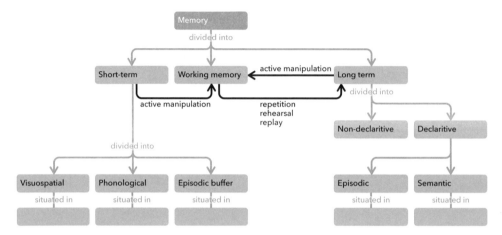

Variations

Optional: You can ask students to present their concept maps to the other groups in an elevator pitch (see ILA Elevator Pitch on page 47) or another short presentation method. Ask the other students to provide feedback on the concept map and have one of the presenters take notes (these can be helpful to update the concept map later).

Optional (only if you also decided to do the presentations): Ask the students to process the feedback of step 3. This could result in additional concepts and relations in their concept map.

References

Structure of the concept map: www.lucidchart.com/pages/concept-map

The framework of this ILA is derived from the curricular design within the Institute for Interdisciplinary Studies.

11 Elevator pitch

Overview

A shared vision is an important driver for collaborative efforts. In order to be able to form an overarching vision for an academic project, students need to be able to express their own vision clearly and effectively within a short period of time. In this learning activity they learn how to do this by focusing on: 1) the most important elements of their vision; 2) using their voice and body language to convince their audience.

Interdisciplinary skills	Ordering and structuring, reasoning and situation awareness		
Characteristics	workshop	course	curriculum
	individual	group	
Duration – activity	45 minutes		
Intended learning outcome	Students are able to explain their vision on an academic project clearly and effectively within two minutes.		
Remarks			

Setup

a Preparation teacher

Tell the students about this assignment in advance of the seminar. Explain the important elements of public speaking (e.g. speaking dynamics, rhythm, use of metaphor/example, importance of repetition, etc.). They will need at least two days to prepare for it.

b Preparation student

Instructions: The elevator pitch
Prepare a talk lasting no more than two minutes, in which you clearly explain your most recent individual academic project. The rest of the group should not be familiar

(or as familiar) with the topic of this project.
The presentation should not include slides or other multimedia. Encourage students to practise with other students from unrelated courses or with their parents to identify 'sticking points', where additional explanation is needed to elucidate their point.

c   Teaching setup
Step 1
At the beginning of the class, repeat the important elements of public speaking (e.g. speaking dynamics, rhythm, use of metaphor/example, importance of repetition, etc.). Also inform the students that they will be expected to provide feedback on their peers' presentations (see the assessment).

Step 2
Organize the order of presentations and start the pitches. Time them carefully – don't be lenient. The time constraint is what forces the students to stay focused and be succinct.

Step 3
Between pitches, have students in the audience provide feedback to the student on his/her public speaking skills and the content: What was clear? What was not clear? Why were things unclear? Did the speaker manage to engage the public and capture their interest in the topic discussed – and why (not)?

Step 4
Discuss differences between an academic presentation and an elevator pitch with the students. In what context could an elevator pitch be more useful? Why?

Variations

When introducing the assignment to students, you could give an elevator pitch yourself.

First-year students may not have a project to talk about. If they don't, you could have them talk about a secondary-school project, or focus their pitches on their personality and what they are planning to learn from a course in the first year.
As a twist, you could repeat this assignment in the last seminar of the course. There, you could have the students focus their pitches on what they have learnt during the course and how their (disciplinary) skills contributed to it.
Videotaping the pitches can be useful for giving the students insight into their presentation skills. Videotaping can also help illustrate what the students have learnt during the course.
You can recommend the students to practise their pitch in front of an audience that is unfamiliar with the topic. It could be even more interesting to arrange an audience for the students that is really not familiar with the topic (e.g. contacts from another research department).

Students feed off of each other in brainstorming, so one person's idea might inspire a new one from somebody else. Remind them to capture those thoughts. By writing them down, they'll be ready to share when their time to speak comes up.

References

The framework of this ILA is derived from the curricular design within the Institute for Interdisciplinary Studies.

12 Interdisciplinary debate

Overview

In order to take a different disciplinary perspective on a topic, the interdisciplinary debate challenges students to defend a disciplinary perspective that is not (necessarily) their own. Apart from perspective taking and reasoning, this learning activity also trains evaluation skills, as students have to act as a member of a jury during the debate as well.

Interdisciplinary skills	Perspective taking, reasoning, evaluating		
Characteristics	workshop	course	curriculum
	individual	group	
Duration - activity	60-90 minutes		
Intended learning outcome	Students are able to argue from a different disciplinary perspective than their own during an interdisciplinary debate; Students are able to use powerful argumentation during the debate; Students are able to refine ideas by being encouraged to think broader and more nuanced and to assess arguments critically; Students are able to transform emotions into opinions that are based on rational arguments; Students are able to listen critically to opponents during the debate; Students are able to reach substantive outcomes during the debate.		
Remarks	Let the students read two academic articles prior to the lecture.		

Setup

a   Preparation teacher

Select and read two academic articles for the students to read before this interdisciplinary learning activity. Prepare statements.

b   Preparation student

Students read the academic articles (the basic input for the debate).

c   Teaching setup

Step 1 (5 minutes)

Introduce a statement based on the literature that the students have read in preparation for this seminar.

Step 2 (10 minutes)

Form two groups. One group is in favour of the statement; the second group argues against it. Ideally you let the students who are 'in favour' represent the 'against' group and vice versa. When choosing a jury of students, form two groups of 4-9 students and one group of five students. These five students are the jury.

Step 3

Give the groups time to prepare for the debate by sharing their views on the provided literature (which should have been read prior to the seminar). The debating groups have to try to find as many arguments for their position as possible and anticipate the possible counter-arguments.

Tip: Based on the Miniature Guide to Critical Thinking (Paul & Elder, 2009), De Greef, Post, Vink and Wenting (2017) created the following guiding questions for interdisciplinary education (see next page). You could let the students use these questions to prepare the discussion.

Elements of thought	Guiding questions for students
All reasoning has a purpose	What am I trying to accomplish? How is interdisciplinarity involved here?
All reasoning is an attempt to figure out something, to settle some question, to solve some problem	What question am I addressing? Do I consider the complexities in the question?
All reasoning is based on data, information and evidence	What information do I need to settle the question? Which methods or disciplines are needed?
All reasoning is expressed through – and shaped by – concepts and ideas	How did I reach this conclusion? Is there another way to interpret the information?
All reasoning contains inferences by which we draw conclusions and give meaning to data	What is the main idea here? Can I explain it?
All reasoning is based on assumptions	What am I taking for granted? What assumption has led me to that conclusion?
All reasoning leads somewhere and has implications and consequences	If someone accepted my position, what would be the implications? What am I implying?
All reasoning is done from some point of view	From what point of view am I looking at this issue? Is there another point of view I should consider? Are all disciplinary perspectives thoroughly looked at?

Elements of thought and guiding questions based on The Miniature Guide to Critical Thinking (Paul & Elder, 2009)

Instruct the jury to pay particular attention to the rhetorical structure of the arguments presented by the debating groups. The jury should attempt to categorize the types of arguments (methodological, theoretical) within each text to anticipate those to be used by the debating groups. The jury should also prepare an introduction to the debate to summarize the positions of both articles.

Explain to the debaters that listening is as important as speaking in a discussion. Unless they listen carefully, they cannot contribute to the stated purpose of communication and only then will they be able to pick up the thread of discussion and continue.

Step 5

Start the debate.
A possible timeline of the debate is:

• Introduction (jury)	2-3 minutes
• Argument group 1	2-4 minutes
• Argument group 2	2-4 minutes
• Discussion	10-20 minutes
• Reaction group 1	1 minute
• Reaction group 2	1 minute
• Conclusion (jury)	5 minutes

Step 6 (10 minutes)

Following the debate, the jury analyses the nature of the conflicting insights and provides a rationale for their choice of the winner.

Assessment

You could grade the students for their debating and listening skills. If you like, you could discuss the presented grading rubric with the jury. An example of a rubric is presented on page 54. You could choose to grade a person or to grade a group.

Dimension	Suggestions for evaluation	Evaluation					Comments
		- -	-	-/+	+	++	
Power of arguments (20%)	Are arguments persuasive?						
	Are arguments connected to scientific literature?						
	Do arguments catch on with the audience?						
	Do(es) the debater(s) draw connections between arguments and existing ideas on an issue?						
Refinement of ideas (20%)	Do arguments encourage broader and more nuanced thinking?						
	Are arguments critically assessed?						
Empathy (10%)	Do arguments show evidence of empathy?						
Rationality (10%)	Are emotions transformed into opinions that are based on rational arguments?						
Critical listening (20%)	Do(es) the debater(s) listen critically to opponents?						
Substantive outcomes (20%)	Do(es) the debater(s)s contribute to analysis of the problem?						
	Do(es) s/he/they provide insight into what we do and don't know?						
	Do(es) the debater(s) expose inconsistencies, generalizations and blind spots?						

Example

Human and animal cognition

Background

Questions about differences between human and animal cognition are hotly debated in various academic fields. Some academics focus on cognitive similarities and state that the cognitive abilities of animals and humans can be placed on a continuum. Other academics suggest that there is a qualitative break between the cognitive functions and abilities of animals and humans and take the differences in neural structures as a point of departure.

Step 1

To prepare for their seminar, students read two texts on human and animal cognition. One text stresses the continuity between human and animal cognition and pleads for a bottom-up approach (De Waal, 2010). The other focuses on the discontinuity in cognitive abilities (Premack, 2007).

Step 2

During the class, the students had to debate the following statement: 'Humans are unique in their cognitive abilities.' The group was divided into three. One group was in favour of the statement and used the text that stresses discontinuity to finalize their arguments and prepare for the debate. Another group was against the statement and used the other article to do the same. The jury used both texts to analyse the source of the differences between the statements and find a way to categorize the different arguments that would probably be brought up during the debate.

Step 3 + 4

Instruct the students (see setup).

Step 5

The chairman of the (group-appointed) jury introduced and led the debate, while other members of the jury took notes and categorized the arguments.

Step 6

After the debate, the jury withdrew in order to summarize the most important arguments and analysed the nature of conflicting insights. In this case, the differences were at a number of levels: the chosen approach to look at the problem (bottom up vs. top down), the types of examples used to support the claims (examples of complex cognitive tasks versus simple cognitive tasks) and the methodology proposed to investigate the topic (focus on cognitive behaviour and abilities versus focus on the neural basis of cognition) were used as points of contention by both groups. The jury eventually evaluated the debate based on the quality of the logic presented in the arguments, and provided this rationale for their choice of a winner.

Variations

An additional task that could be proposed to the students is to have both groups present an experiment or methodology with which to find a solution to the statement. In the above example, this would have meant having to present a method to assess whether humans are unique in their cognitive capabilities. After both presentations, the jury could react to and discuss the proposals.

To complicate matters further (for advanced groups), in their conclusion the jury could also introduce a third (disciplinary) perspective on the matter.

References

The framework of this ILA is derived from the curricular design within the Institute for Interdisciplinary Studies.

- Greef, L. de, Post, G., Vink, C., Wenting, L. (2017). *Designing Interdisciplinary Education: a practical handbook for university teachers.* Amsterdam, Amsterdam University Press.
- Paul, R., & Elder, L. (2009). *The miniature guide to critical thinking: Concepts and tools* (6th ed.). Dillon Beach, CA: Foundation for Critical Thinking.
- Premack, D. (2007). Human and Animal Cognition: Continuity and Discontinuity, *PNAS*, 104(35), 13861-13867.
- Waal, de F. & Ferrari, P.F. (2010). Towards a bottom-up perspective on animal and human cognition, *Trends in Cognitive Sciences*, 14(5), 201-207.

13 Personal strengths matrix

Overview

Before starting a group project, it is useful for students to get to know one another, set the ground rules, establish roles and responsibilities and to be aware of each other's strengths and pitfalls. Therefore, students fill in a personal strengths matrix, in which they write down their core strength(s), pitfall(s), allergies (peeves) and challenges. This personal strengths matrix is the starting point for a group dialogue.

Interdisciplinary skills	Reflection, shared leadership, situation awareness		
Characteristics	workshop	course	curriculum
	individual	group	
Duration – activity	45 minutes		
Intended learning outcome	Students are able to reflect on their strengths and pitfalls by filling in the personal strengths matrix. Students are able to discuss their strengths and pitfalls with their peers.		
Remarks	The personal strengths matrix on paper (one matrix per student)		

Setup

a   Preparation teacher

This learning activity helps students to reflect on their personal strengths and pitfalls, and is most valuable at the beginning of a course in which students have to work together in groups. For example, when students are going to do research, a research project or work on a case study together.

Prepare a presentation in which you explain the personal strengths matrix and focus on the different aspects of the matrix. In addition, print a strengths matrix for every student to fill in during the lecture.

Tip: Make sure that you create a positive and safe group atmosphere before starting this ILA.

b   Teaching setup
Step 1
Start the lecture with a presentation about the strengths matrix. It is important to visualize the matrix during this presentation (on a flip chart or slide). You start with the core strength and explain the model clockwise (A-B-C-D). If you feel comfortable, you could fill in one matrix about yourself and explain this to the students.

A. Core strength	B. Pitfall
■ What other appreciate about me ■ What I take for granted with myself ■ What I expect from others	■ What is disturbing to others? ■ What I accept from other people ■ What I justify
C. Allergy	D. Challenge
■ What I dislike in others ■ What I least want to be myself	■ What I lack in myself ■ What I need to work in ■ What I wish I had ■ What I admire in other people

Step 2
Give all the students a matrix and ask them to fill it in. If you observe that students are having a hard time explaining their strengths, you could also start in small groups and let the students help each other to formulate their strengths. It is important that they only help with the strengths, and that they individually fill in the other three parts of the matrix.

Step 3
Make groups of approximately four students. If they have to work together for an assignment, it is important to also work in this particular group during this learning activity. Let them discuss their personal matrices. By doing this, students become aware of the strengths and pitfalls of their group members, and could discuss beforehand how they could avoid conflicts related to the personal strengths matrices.

Example
You'll find an example of a filled-in matrix from a teacher below. A filled-in matrix and your personal experiences help students to fill in their own forms. You can use this matrix to give examples of your own teamwork experiences.

A. Core strength	B. Pitfall
A good listener	**Passivity in groups**
C. Allergy	D. Challenge
Too dominant	**To show assertivity in groups**

Variations

If students work together for a longer period of time, you could schedule some feedback moments (for example using the OEPS model, see the ILA on page 132) in which they discuss their teamwork using the matrices.

You can use the students' matrices (and yours) to discuss how you as a teacher and the students would like to collaborate. You can discuss the values that are important to you (i.e. respect, honesty, support).

If students struggle to fill in the matrix, they can use the table below to give them more insights into their teamwork skills.

References

The framework of this ILA is derived from the curricular design within the Institute for Interdisciplinary Studies.
The matrix was developed by Daniël Ofman.

14 Shuffling teams

Overview

Students start in groups with others who have a similar or the same disciplinary background and discuss an answer to a specific research question. When all the groups have formulated an answer, they are shuffled from disciplinary into interdisciplinary teams, and they have to come up with an interdisciplinary answer. This process will help students to see pros and cons of (inter)disciplinary research.

Interdisciplinary skills	Evaluating, formulating a common goal, a questioning attitude		
Characteristics	workshop	course	curriculum
	individual	group	
Duration - activity	45-60 minutes		
Intended learning outcome	Students are able to discuss a question from their own discipline and find an interdisciplinary solution together with students from other disciplines.		
Remarks	You could either do this ILA with interdisciplinary students with a major in a specific discipline, or in a course in which students from several disciplines come together.		

Setup

a   Preparation teacher

Find a case/ problem suitable for your course.

b   Teaching setup

Step 1

Introduce the case/problem to the students.

Tip: Let the students read a paper on the topic before the start of this activity.

Step 2
Divide the students into groups of 3-5 students and make sure students with the same or similar disciplinary backgrounds form groups (i.e. biology students together with biology students, psychology students together with psychology students).

Step 3
Ask each group to generate questions about how the problem could be interpreted and answered from their specific disciplinary perspective. Let them come up with questions, methods, concepts and theories related to their discipline.

Step 4
After the groups have generated these questions, disperse the groups, and assign students to work with students from other groups – thus creating interdisciplinary teams.

Step 5
Ask students to discuss the case again and come up with an integrated solution by evaluating and comparing the different disciplinary answers.

Step 6
Invite one student of each group to present their integrated solution to the problem. If you would like to have short presentations, you could use the activity 'Elevator Pitch' (see page 47).

Step 7
Discuss the differences between the questions and answers from the disciplinary and interdisciplinary teams in a plenary session. After this discussion, ask the students to reflect on the process by answering the following two questions:
1   Was it helpful to approach this problem/case from an interdisciplinary perspective? And why (not)?
2   Was it difficult to work with students and information from other disciplines? And why (not)?

Example
Example of a case/problem you can use: Peaceful versus belligerent societies.
In an 'Evolutionary Thinking' course, students are challenged to think about explanations for the existence of both peaceful and belligerent societies. Four teams are formed and each team reads a different article on peaceful and belligerent societies. One team learns about an anthropological perspective on the evolution of human aggression; another team focuses on population genetics from the perspective of theoretical biology; the third team reads a text in which a behavioural biologist perspective leads to the conclusion that 'humans crave violence just like sex'; and the fourth team discusses a sociological text on the nature of peaceful or nonviolent societies.

Within each team, the following questions are discussed:
- What explanation for the existence of peaceful and belligerent societies is given?
- To what extent is the given explanation an evolutionary explanation and can it be linked to a 'VSR' algorithm?
  - V = what varies, and of which characteristic is this a variation?
  - S = what kind of circumstance (natural, social, sexual, cultural, mixed) causes the selection of that characteristic?
  - R = how is this variation reproduced in next generations?

After a fifteen-minute discussion, the teams disperse and reform into new teams comprised of one student from each of the previous teams, thus ensuring different disciplinary perspectives. During the second fifteen-minute discussion, each student presents the reasoning of his/her previous (disciplinary) group. The group then synthesizes new points regarding the existence of peaceful and belligerent societies.

Within each team, the following questions could be discussed:
- What explains the existence of peaceful and belligerent societies?
- Which explanations are more convincing than others?
- Which explanations are complementary?
- Which explanations are contradictory?

Variations

If the level of the disciplinary expertise of the students is sufficiently high, it may not be necessary to provide a complex problem. Instead, after having identified the students' variety of disciplinary backgrounds, have them generate as a group a complex problem for which they, again as a group, would like to find an integrated (interdisciplinary) solution.

If you don't wish to finish this ILA with a group discussion comprising mini-presentations of integrative solutions by each interdisciplinary team, you could have the students return to their original (disciplinary) teams so that they can inform their former group of the outcomes of the discussion.

References

The framework of this ILA is derived from the curricular design within the Institute for Interdisciplinary Studies.

15 Team charter

Overview

To facilitate a productive collaboration, it can help for team members to be aware of their strong and weak points. Team charters not only make these explicit, but also encourage discussions between team members on their shared vision and what they consider a successful end result. Moreover, the charters facilitate collaborative skills, as the charters can be input for giving feedback and reflections on team processes. The team charter is a good starting point for group assignments (e.g. research projects).

Interdisciplinary skills	Reflection, shared leadership, formulating a common goal		
Characteristics	workshop	course	curriculum
	individual	group	
Duration - activity	60 minutes		
Intended learning outcome	Students are able to reflect on what they can contribute to a team by filling in a team charter; Students are able to discuss in a small group of peers their strong and weak points regarding teamwork.		
Remarks			

Setup

a   Preparation teacher

Complete the team charter boxes with your own strong and weak points. Divide the students into groups for the assignment.

Tip: Make sure that you create a positive and safe group atmosphere before starting this ILA.

Teaching setup

Step 1

Start the first meeting of the course with this ILA. Explain the boxes to the students.

My success	What do others need to know about me
What do I need	What do I add

- At the top left, the student starts with 'my success'. When do you consider a project a success?
- At the top right, the student writes down 'what do the others need to know about me?'. Here the student writes down his/her points for improvement.
- At the bottom left, the student writes down what s/he needs from other team members, by answering the question: what helps me to successfully finish the project?
- At the bottom right, the student writes down 'what do I add?'. This is where they write down their strong points and what they can add to a team.

Step 2

Show your own filled-in team charter as an example. If possible, show how the charter has helped you in previous team collaborations.

Step 3

Ask the students to fill in their strong and weak points in the four boxes of their own charter. They can draw the scheme on paper themselves, use a form on their computer, or you could give them a printed scheme.

Step 4

Invite the group members to share their individual schemes, and create one scheme combining the information from all team members. Monitor the atmosphere while walking around. It is important to lead the conversation when the atmosphere in a group starts to become unpleasant.

Step 5

The groups make agreements on how they will work together as a team for the coming weeks, based on these filled-in schemes. They can make agreements on ground rules, for example, how they want to give each other feedback (on assignments), what the expectations are regarding attendance, how many times the team members will meet, how they will keep each other informed. And on tasks, such as who will be in charge of filtering out spelling mistakes in assignments, the structure of the assignments, the presentation of the work, meeting the deadlines, etc.

The team charters and the agreements are documented and preserved by a group member, who is appointed the process leader. S/he makes sure that the documents are available at every meeting. Moreover, the process leader intervenes as soon as the group members do not cooperate properly during the project.

Step 6
Once a week the students evaluate their progress. They use the schemes to evaluate their contribution and make appointments for the coming week.

Example
Examples of filled-in forms by other teachers

My success	What do others need to know about me
■ Humour	■ I am critical
■ Hard-working co-workers	■ Sometimes I am too bossy

What do I need	What do I add
■ Critical co-workers	■ Leadership
■ Contradiction	■ Deadlines

My success	What do others need to know about me
■ Humour	■ Sometimes I finish my work too late
■ Compliments about my work	■ I am a bit lazy

What do I need	What do I add
■ Deadlines	■ Knowledge of the German, Dutch and English language
■ Feedback	■ Knowledge of Windows, Excel and SPSS
	■ A team player

Variations

As with the personal strength matrix, you can use the students' team charters (and yours) to discuss how you and students can collaborate. For this purpose, you can specifically discuss 'what do I need' and 'what do I add' in your team charter.

References

The framework of this ILA is derived from the pressure-cooker programme within the Institute for Interdisciplinary Studies.

16 Strengths game

Overview

Collaboration benefits from insights into the strengths and weaknesses of the team members. In this learning activity students learn what their strengths and personal development points are, and are able to help others become aware of their strengths and weaknesses.

Interdisciplinary skills	Reflection, shared leadership, perspective taking		
Characteristics	workshop	course	curriculum
	individual	group	
Duration - activity	60 minutes		
Intended learning outcome	Students are able to reflect on personal strengths and weaknesses in a group context; Students are able to give and receive feedback on personal traits		
Remarks	Cards with the strengths and weaknesses (one set of cards per group).		

Setup

a Preparation teacher

Prepare a hand out or a PowerPoint slide with the rules of the game.

b Teaching setup

Step 1

Let the students form groups of four.

Step 2

Present the rules of round one of the game. You can give all groups a handout or prepare a PowerPoint slide. Tell the students that they will all end the game with two strengths they think fit them best.

Rules of the game: round one
1 Every student starts with five random cards. Any remaining cards are shuffled and presented on a stack with the strengths facing down.
2 When it is your turn, you will pick one card from the stack, which means you'll have six cards.
3 Choose the card that least reflects your strengths.
   a You have two options:
   b Place this card in front of another student if you think this strength fits him or her. Explain why you think this is the case. The receiver of the card may ask questions.
4 Place the card on a (new) stack with strengths that doesn't fit any of the players.
5 Step 1 till 4 continue until the stack is finished.
6 Now place all the cards you received (either from the stack or from other students) in front of you.
7 Discuss every student's cards. What did you observe? Are there any strengths related to each other?
8 End the game with your personal selection of two cards reflecting your strengths best. Write down these strengths.

Step 3

Every student now has two cards with strengths. However, it is also important to reflect on your weaknesses. Therefore, present the rules of round two.
Rules of the game: round two
1 Place all the cards with the 'weaknesses' on the table
2 When it's your turn, pick the card that reflects your weakness best. Tell the other students why this is your weakness and try to convince them (you could give examples). This way, all students will get a card which suits them best.
3 The game ends when every student has one card and everyone agrees on the match between student and weakness.

Step 4

End the tutorial with an evaluation of the two rounds. You could ask students the following questions:
■ Was it hard to think about your own strengths and weaknesses?
■ Was it hard to think about strengths and weaknesses of your fellow students?
■ Which round was easier, one or two?

Example

Examples of a set of cards for round one and round two.

Knows how to convince other people
Persistent
Attentive
Purposive
Responsible
Tidy
Curious
Mediator
Knows how to distinguish oneself
Powerful
Ambitious
Knowledgeable
Balanced
Dedicated
Can put things into perspective
Easy-going
Practical
Disciplined
Idealistic
Organizer
Adventurous
Spontaneous
Flexible
Identifies connections
Helpful
Content
Punctual
Consistent
Inspiring
Humorous
Sensitive
Independent
Bright
Respectful
Robust

Cards for round two:

Inconsistent attitude
Indifferent
Egocentric
Undisciplined
Poorly concentrated
Too much focused on others (at the cost of own needs)
Passive
Overactive
Difficulties with teamwork
Pessimist
Lazy
Overbearing
Bossy
Stubborn
Bad listener

(Students can add a new card, if none of the above formulated weaknesses fits)

Tip: This game only works if all students take it seriously and really try to help each other. To support this, students who have worked together on a (research) project before, and therefore know each other, can form a group.

Variations

You could follow up this game with the learning activity of the strength matrix (see page 57). The students could start with their strength(s) gathered in round one of the game.

References

The framework of this ILA is derived from the curricular design within the Institute for Interdisciplinary Studies.

17 Walt Disney strategy

Overview

The Walt Disney strategy stimulates creative thinking, for example when students need to come up with solutions for complex problems. First students are challenged to have an open and positive attitude in order to come up with new and unconventional ideas. Then students are stimulated to translate their ideas into structured and concrete plans.

Interdisciplinary skills	A questioning attitude, formulating a common goal, analysing		
Characteristics	workshop	course	curriculum
	individual	group	
Duration – activity	90 minutes		
Intended learning outcome	Students are able to come up with at least ten possible solutions for complex problems; Students are able to use the central question to specify a creative solution; Students are able to give feedback on the feasibility of an idea.		
Remarks	You need three imagined or real rooms, flip charts, markers.		

Setup

a   Preparation teacher

Make sure you have three separate rooms available for this workshop. If it is not possible to have three separate rooms, create three different divisions in one room, in order to differentiate between the dream room, the reality room and the sweatbox.

Teaching setup
Step 1

Present the students with a case, a problem or a research question. Then divide the class into smaller groups of 6-7 students.

Step 2

Direct the students to the **dream room** (this may be an actual room or just a part of the classroom). In the dream room ideas are being created. Explain that everything is possible – there are no boundaries. Ask the students to write down every idea on a Post-it, which they then stick on a large piece of paper. When everyone has finished his/her ideas, let the students walk around and provide feedback on the ideas. Only positive feedback (comments like 'great idea' etc.) is allowed in the dream room.

Step 3

After the dream room, direct the students to the **reality room**. In this room they pick one or more ideas that were generated in the dream room to further elaborate upon. The goal is to translate their idea into a structured and concrete plan. The central question in the reality room is: 'How does it work?' Or: 'How do we make it work?' Encourage the students to remain positive about the possibilities but also to be precise and as concrete as possible.

Step 4

The next room is the **sweatbox**. In this room, students pitch their idea to the rest of the group (see also elevator pitch on page 47). The group gives feedback on each other's ideas, guided by the question: 'Is this possible?'

Example

How to solve low levels of work motivation?
In a course on labour & organization, students from various backgrounds (psychology, sociology and business studies) were challenged to think creatively about a research design that would enable them to solve a real-life problem. A medium-sized international company based in Amsterdam was struggling with low levels of motivation amongst its employees. The main question that had to be investigated with their research design was: 'What causes the low levels of motivation among employees?'

In the **dream room**, students came up with many ideas, based on their knowledge from different fields and different perspectives on the focus of the problem. Some examples of these ideas were: ask the employees to keep a diary about their experiences at work; perform a discourse analysis on their work emails; start working undercover and observe what's going on; ask them to do something completely different for two days and evaluate the changes; use focus groups; switch jobs among the employees and reverse power relations as an experiment; take them on a trip; and do personality tests.

In the **reality room**, the students took a closer look at their ideas and found that although most of the ideas were not realistic, they touched upon important aspects of work motivation. The lack of motivation could have something to do with personality, power relations, type of work, type of organization, and/or the reward system. In order to keep all options open, they chose an explorative approach. Employees from different levels within the organization were asked to keep a journal for one week and to write about their experiences at work. They were given the freedom in the structure and length of their reflections, but were asked to address the highlights and low points of each day.

After they had presented this idea to the rest of the group in the **sweatbox**, peers gave feedback on how to approach the employees, ensure anonymity, and present the results to the organization. The group also suggested that the research would need a second phase in order to answer the research question.

Variations

To prepare the students for the dream room, you could do a brief exercise in which they experience the differences between stimulating and resisting ideas. Divide the students into pairs and for two minutes, have one member of each pair propose all kinds of ideas, to which the other member always responds 'No'; after one minute this student switches to positive and enthusiastic reactions. Change roles after two minutes.

The setup of the three (imagined or real) rooms can promote the purpose of the stage the students are in. The following are examples of possible setups:

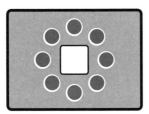 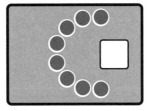 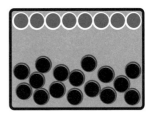

Dream room	Reality room	Sweatbox
the group is arranged in a circle around the ideas they come up with.	the group is arranged in a half-circle and they are facing the ideas they picked to work out.	the group is confronted with the rest of the group, who will critically analyse their idea.

References

The framework of this ILA is derived from the curricular design within the Psychology Department of the University of Amsterdam.

18 A closer look at interdisciplinary texts

Overview

Students learn strategies for writing (and evaluating) an interdisciplinary essay by using interdisciplinary writing guidelines and giving and receiving guided peer feedback. This learning activity is mainly focused on training students' critical-thinking skills.

Interdisciplinary skills	Reasoning, analysing, evaluating		
Characteristics	workshop	course	curriculum
	individual	group	
Duration – activity	90 minutes		
Intended learning outcome	Students are able to write an interdisciplinary essay that meets the criteria of purposefulness, disciplinary grounding, integration and critical awareness; Students are able to give substantiated feedback on the essays of peers by using an assessment rubric.		
Remarks			

Setup

a   Preparation teacher

Organize two seminars about a topic that has been thoroughly studied by at least two well-known academics with different disciplinary backgrounds. The assignment ideally takes place over the course of two seminars with a two-week gap between them.

Read the article by Boix Mansilla et al. (2009) to get background information on the criteria and develop a rubric that the students can use for the peer assessment.

b   Preparation student
The students attend the two seminars and study the academic papers selected by the lecturer before the seminar.

c   Teaching setup
Step 1
At the first meeting explain the goal of the assignment. The goal of this assignment is to write an interdisciplinary essay (around 1,000 words) about the topic the lecturer chooses by integrating the insights of two academics and to give feedback on an essay of a peer using the following guidelines:

1   Purposefulness: The degree to which a student is able to provide clarity in his/her academic text about the aims and audience of their interdisciplinary writing;
2   Disciplinary grounding: The student's ability to select, understand and use empirical literature from multiple disciplines to inform his or her work;
3   Integration: The student's ability to explain how perspectives come across in the chosen literature, to identify connections across disciplines and to synthesize these points into a coherent whole;
4   Critical awareness: The student's capacity to take a meta-disciplinary perspective on his or her interdisciplinary work and to reflect upon the craft of weaving disciplines together.

Next, introduce the topic. After the introduction instruct the students to formulate a leading question regarding this topic and then attempt to answer this question in an essay in which they try to integrate the insights from the two academics. Ask the students to bring their essay to the next tutorial.

Step 2
All students bring their essay to class. Explain that the goal of this meeting is to give written and oral feedback on an essay of a peer using the guidelines. Explain the guidelines again and introduce the different levels on which you can master these guidelines. Then divide the students in pairs and ask them to exchange their essays. Instruct the students to read the essays and first give written feedback. After the students are finished ask them to explain their feedback orally. To close the learning activity, discuss their personal experiences of completing this assignment in a plenary session. Focus this discussion on the four guidelines.

d   Assessment
See Appendix on page 163.

Example
Interdisciplinary writing on alienation
A short introduction is given about the different perspectives that Marx, Weber, Durkheim and Simmel used when describing alienation in modern society (e.g. Calhoun's [2012] 'Classical and Contemporary Sociological Theory Readers' provides a good overview of this debate).
The students are then asked to write a 1,000-word essay that combines the

perspectives addressed in the literature on alienation. In their essays, the students may elaborate on the fact that the concerns of the four academics about modern society are what binds them together despite the differences in their assumptions, their ideas about the cause, their ideas about the scale to which alienation represents itself and their ideas about the possible consequences. Note that the disciplinary grounding of these social scientists might be difficult to identify in this example. At the second seminar, the students exchange peer reviews of their essays, then discuss their experiences of writing the essay and the direction it could have taken. This discussion could include suggestions regarding how to have best tackled the topic.

Variations

Make the assignment easier by providing the question that the students should answer in their essay and the two articles that students should use. After practising a few times, students can formulate their own question.

Another option for making this assignment easier is to use interdisciplinary texts to answer the question instead of disciplinary texts.

To increase the challenge of interdisciplinary writing, ask the students to elaborate the information in their essays that is derived from a third discipline.

To add a further challenge (for a particularly advanced group), say that the essay could be based on the work of two or more academics who studied various topics and ask the students to integrate these diverse topics into a unified whole.

Add a third seminar in which the students rewrite their essays incorporating the feedback they received from their peers during the second seminar. The teacher could grade these essays.

References

The framework of this ILA is derived from the curricular design within the Association for Integrative Studies.

The example of this ILA was developed by teachers of Interdisciplinary Social Sciences at the University of Amsterdam.

- Boix Mansilla, V., Dawes Duraisingh, E., Wolfe, C.R., Haynes, C. (2009a). Targeted Assessment Rubric: An Empirically Grounded Rubric for Interdisciplinary Writing, *The Journal of Higher Education*, 80(3), 334-353.
- Calhoun, C. (2012). *Classical and Contemporary Sociological Theory Readers*, John Wiley & Sons Inc.: Hoboken, New Jersey.

19 Complex systems

Overview

Students learn to collaboratively analyse complex systems by first focusing on each specific element, then identifying the relations between different elements and combining each other's knowledge.

Interdisciplinary skills	Ordering and structuring, analysing, shared leadership		
Characteristics	workshop	course	curriculum
	individual	group	
Duration – activity	90 minutes		
Intended learning outcome	Students are able to analyse a specific level or agent in a complex system; Students are able to identify the relationships between different elements in a complex system; Students are able to create a model of a complex system by synthesizing each other's knowledge on the different levels or agents.		
Remarks	Flip chart and coloured markers are needed.		

Setup

a   Preparation teacher

Prepare a complex problem or topic by collecting different academic papers describing the different levels or agents constituting this problem and how these levels or agents are interconnected. There are four basic factors that are essential for a system to be classified as complex (Menken & Keestra, 2017):

1   The presence of a collection of diverse agents (i.e. atoms, molecules, hooligans);
2   These agents have to be interconnected and their behaviour and actions have to be interdependent (i.e. they must form a network);

3   The collection of agents tends to self-organize as a result of feedback and
    feed-forward loops between agents;
4   The agents must be able to adapt to change or learn;
In the section example from a teacher's perspective you can find an example of
complex problems with different levels of agents. Select at least one that students
have to read to prepare for this activity.

Divide the students into groups of 3-4 students. The number of groups should
correspond to the number of agents or levels that are identified within the system.
If possible, take into account the disciplinary backgrounds of the students when
making the groups. Integration will be facilitated if students have to work together
with students with different backgrounds.

b   Preparation student
The student should read at least one academic paper about a complex problem or
topic that is selected by the teacher.

Tip: Do not forget self-study time. It may be helpful to create a sheet or assignment
for students including the intended learning outcomes they are required to meet by
the end of the self-study time.

c   Teaching setup
        Step 1
Introduce the complex problem or topic. Show the different levels or agents within
the particular system. Explain that the goal of this seminar is to collaboratively
analyse the system related to this topic/problem by combining their knowledge and
to identify the relationships between the different agents or levels.

Step 2
Assign each group to a specific level or agent in the system. Explain that each group
has fifteen minutes to understand their level or agent in the system. Instruct the
students to visualize the processes that take place at their level of analysis on the
provided poster-sized paper.

Step 3
After fifteen minutes, collect the posters and present them at the front of the room.
Invite each group to present their poster and discuss the poster with the class.

Step 4
Explain to the students that they are going to identify and visualize interconnections
and relations between the different levels/agents of the whole system. Ask the
students to identify the feedback loops that are present in the system by discussing
how the processes at each level influence processes at another level.
After this explanation, instruct the students to form new groups, where in each
group there is one representative of each level/agent.

Step 5

After fifteen minutes, invite the groups to present their system to the class. Have a group discussion about the relations and feedback loops in the system. Construct with the group a model of the system based on the collaborative analysis.

d   Assessment

Level E	Level D	Level C	Level B	Level A
None of the four aspects are present:	One of the four aspects is present:	Two of the four aspects are present:	Three of the four aspects are present:	All aspects are present:
1. All levels and agents are represented in the model. A short description of each level/agents is given.	1. All levels and agents are represented in the model. A short description of each level/agents is given.	1. All levels and agents are represented in the model. A short description of each level/agents is given.	1. All levels and agents are represented in the model. A short description of each level/agents is given.	1. All levels and agents are represented in the model. A short description of each level/agents is given.
2. The inter-connections between the different processes are visualized and described correctly in the paper.	2. The inter-connections between the different processes are visualized and described correctly in the paper.	2. The inter-connections between the different processes are visualized and described correctly in the paper.	2. The inter-connections between the different processes are visualized and described correctly in the paper.	2. The inter-connections between the different processes are visualized and described correctly in the paper.
3. Feedback loops in the system are identified and described.	3. Feedback loops in the system are identified and described.	3. Feedback loops in the system are identified and described.	3. Feedback loops in the system are identified and described.	3. Feedback loops in the system are identified and described.
4. The effects of interventions on one level are correctly described on another level.	4. The effects of interventions on one level are correctly described on another level.	4. The effects of interventions on one level are correctly described on another level	4. The effects of interventions on one level are correctly described on another level	4. The effects of interventions on one level are correctly described on another level

Complex systems
Examples of complex problems/topics are described as multilevel systems:

Brains:
In the brains neurons are the agents that pass on signals to each other and form an interconnected network of billions of neurons. Due to this network the property of consciousness emerges. In this network studies separate different levels of agents: molecular, cellular, circuit (groups of cells), systems (functional groups of circuits), whole-brain and embodied levels (embodied means that the brain is seen as operating in the context of a body and an environment).

Slime moulds:
Slime moulds have an internal biochemistry that maintains their cellular integrity, they are microorganisms at the cellular scale, and they are self-organized units at the multicellular (collective) scale. Slime moulds operate, as collectives, in an ecology of foodstuff and danger.

Cities:
A city is also a collection of different agents with daily flows of goods, people living their daily lives and the organization of its infrastructure. It is a self-organizing system, because it functions even without a city planner.

Corporations:
Corporations are made up of departments, which in turn are made up of divisions that consist of individual human beings. In addition, corporations operate in a wider industrial network (of services, goods and waste) and this network operates in the economy as a whole. Note: not all 'levels' are clear-cut in this example. For example, the industrial network and the complete economy operate on the same scale and are both within the domain of macroeconomics.

Variations

For experienced students, add a step 6 in which you ask the students to build a working model of the complex system with a programme. With a working model you could let the student analyse the interplay of different levels in the system.

Add a step 6 where students think of an experiment that intervenes at one of the identified levels. Ask the students: What kind of outcome they expect to see at another level after the intervention at a different level?

If the students are not advanced in working together with students with different disciplinary backgrounds, you could do step 4 and 5 in a plenary session instead of in smaller groups.

If you want to assess the models you could include an assignment where students have to write a short paper on the system, including the relations between different levels/agents and the effects of interventions on the behaviour/outcomes of the system.

References

The framework of this ILA is derived from the curricular design within the Institute for Interdisciplinary Studies.

Craver, C.F. (2002). Interlevel Experiments and Multilevel Mechanisms in the Neuroscience of Memory, *Philosophy of Science*, 69(3), 83-97.

20 Designing an interdisciplinary research question

Overview

Students learn how to use a brainstorm session and a mind map to come up with an interdisciplinary research question and sub-questions on a topic of interest.

Interdisciplinary skills	Sound decision making, situation awareness, ordering and structuring		
Characteristics	workshop	course	curriculum
	individual	group	
Duration – activity	90 minutes		
Intended learning outcome	Students can design an interdisciplinary research question that can be answered by using their different disciplinary backgrounds.		
Remarks	Flip chart for the mind map and research question are needed		

Setup

a   Preparation teacher

The teacher should prepare a presentation with the different steps of the process. The teacher could make the groups (3-4 students) upfront or during the first seminar. Next, the teacher can familiarize him/herself with Socratic questioning and create a handout with more information about Socratic questioning (see the Socratic method on page 41).

b   Preparation student

Ask students to bring at least three examples of complex problems or issues that are important or meaningful to them. You could also let the students familiarize themselves with Socratic questioning before the workshop by letting them read a handout about Socratic questioning.

c   Teaching setup

Step 1: Finding a shared topic of interest

Ask the students to individually write down complex problems or issues that are important and meaningful to them. Next, divide the students into groups of four. Then, ask the students to explore overlapping issues. Let the groups jointly choose one complex problem or issue that they would like to investigate with the group.

Tip: Choose a broad research domain such as sustainability or complexity. This specification will prevent students to spend too much time on selecting a topic.

Step 2: Quick scan of the complex issue

Ask students to individually brainstorm on the problem or issue by noting words, questions, disciplines, techniques, methods and theories that they associate with the chosen issue. After they have finished this, ask them to create their own mind map by distinguishing between the main and secondary elements related to the issue and make connections between the different elements.

Tip: You can emphasize the importance of brainstorming by explaining that it is an activating method that generates many ideas about a particular issue of a topic. A brainstorming session is intended to stimulate out-of-the-box thinking and breaking through fixed mindsets.

Tip: You can emphasize the importance of making a mind map by explaining that in this way you, as it were, externalize the capacity of your working memory in a way that resembles the functioning of your brain. This allows you to structure, comprehend and process more information faster.

Step 3: Differences and similarities in views on a shared topic

When all students have finished their mind map, let them discuss the differences and similarities between their mind maps and reflect upon the reasons for these differences and similarities. Let them write down their findings.

Asking the following questions could assist students in finding the similarities and differences:

- How do the other disciplines investigate your shared research topic? Could their methods, subjects, instruments etc. be added to those of your discipline or do they focus on different components or processes?
- Do you believe that certain components or processes form coherent subcomponents? Or that a certain component should be separated into two or more independent components? Could this explain how the results of a particular study are related to those of a study in another discipline?
- What contextual, external or environmental factor merits more study as it might have a decisive impact on your research topic?

- What developmental or historical episode has been neglected and is relevant for your research topic? Could adding historical elements to an explanatory theory solve this issue?
- What particular intervention might affect your research topic in a decisive way and deserves to be better understood?

Tip: Introduce the students to Socratic questioning. The pedagogy of Socratic questions is open-ended, focusing on broad, general ideas rather than specific, factual information. The questioning technique emphasizes a level of questioning and thinking where there is no single right answer. It generally starts with an open-ended question proposed by one student. The participants have to listen actively in order to respond effectively to what others have contributed. Participants must demonstrate respect for different ideas, thoughts and values, and must not interrupt each other (see also the Socratic method on page 41).

Step 4: Designing a research question
After the discussion, ask the students to draw a common mind map in their group of 3-4 participants. At least one element of each individual mind map should be incorporated, so that every student participates in this step. Ask the students to formulate a main research question and four sub-questions based on their mind map and note which disciplines will help them to answer the main question.

Step 5
The students present their main research question and sub-questions based on the mind map they created. Let the students pitch the reason why they chose this question.
Close the tutorial with a reflection on the process.

d   Assessment
You could use the grading rubric on page 85 to assess the research questions. This grading rubric is adapted from Repko, Szostak & Buchberger (2013).

Grading rubric

Criteria	Yes/No/Incomplete information
The student defines the problem or research question in a way that is appropriate to interdisciplinary study.	
The student clearly defines the scope of the study	
The student avoids the three tendencies that run counter to interdisciplinary process: disciplinary jargon, disciplinary bias and personal bias.	
The student answers the 'so what' question?	

Variations

To help students reflect on the differences and similarities between their mind maps ask the students to write down to which disciplines the elements are related.

You could incorporate the interdisciplinary learning activity 'finding a shared topic of interest' in step 1 (see page 86).

References

This ILA is derived from: Menken, S. & Keestra, M. (2016). *An Introduction to Interdisciplinary Research: Theory and Practice.* Amsterdam University Press, Amsterdam.

- De Greef, L., Post, G., Vink, C., Wenting, L. (2017). *Designing Interdisciplinary Education: a practical handbook for university teachers.* Amsterdam, Amsterdam University Press.
- Repko, A.F., Szostak, R., & Buchberger, M.P. (2013). *Introduction to interdisciplinary studies.* Sage Publications.

21 Finding a shared topic

Overview

Students learn to use the method of triangulation to find a shared topic of interest between different disciplines. This activity can be used as a starting point in an interdisciplinary research project where the team consists of a given combination of disciplines.

Interdisciplinary skills	Situation awareness, formulating a common goal, a questioning attitude		
Characteristics	workshop	course	curriculum
	individual	group	
Duration – activity	Minimum 30 minutes		
Intended learning outcome	Students are able to use the triangulation method to find a shared topic of interest.		
Remarks	You can hand out several triangulation forms.		

Setup

a Preparation teacher

Print the triangulation forms for teams that consist of 3-4 students. Fill in the triangulation form yourself. You can use this as an example in this activity.

b Preparation student

Ask the students to think about topics they would like to study in the project.

Tip: Explain before the workshop that students have to pitch their idea to the group. This can serve as an extra motivation for students.

c   Teaching setup

This activity can be used as a starting point in interdisciplinary research where the team consists of a given combination of disciplines.

Step 1

Explain the goal of this activity by showing an example of a triangulation form. Instruct the students to write down individually a list of topics that they would like to study.

Step 2

Instruct students to exchange the different lists of topics in their research team. Each student has to note several sub-questions her/his discipline could answer for each topic on the list provided by the other students.

Step 3

Invite students to discuss the topic and sub-questions with their team. Ask the students to fill in the triangulation form where each circle represents a topic in a discipline. Where the circles overlap, the students have to write down the subtopic that is studied in both disciplines, in three disciplines or even four disciplines. Suggest to the students that they start with the topic with the most noted sub-questions (in the previous step), because that topic relates to the most subtopics in several disciplines.

Tip: Ask students to do this for the different topics.

Tip: To organize the team discussion, assign the role of chairperson to one student per team. His/her role is to keep the conversation focused on the task and effective.

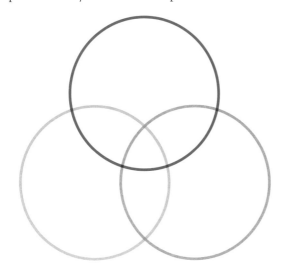

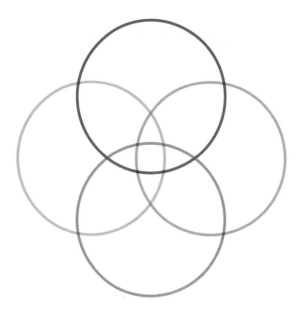

Instruct the students to formulate a common research question and the set of sub-questions based on their shared findings.

Example

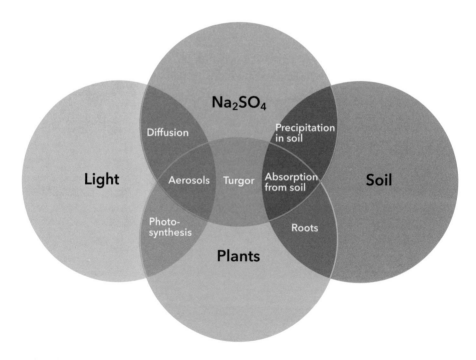

This triangulation shows the subtopics that are shared by the disciplines biology, chemistry, physics and earth sciences. Adapted from Menken & Keestra (2017).

Variations

You could incorporate the interdisciplinary learning activity 'designing a research question' in step 1 (see page 86).

References

This ILA is derived from: Menken, S. & Keestra, M. (2016). *An Introduction to Interdisciplinary Research: Theory and Practice.* Amsterdam University Press, Amsterdam.

22 The interdisciplinary shuttle

Overview

Students learn to design an interdisciplinary research proposal by combining their knowledge and skills. In this activity students are introduced to one another's disciplines and the corresponding strengths and weaknesses.

Interdisciplinary skills	Formulating common goals, reasoning, dealing with cognitive biases		
Characteristics	workshop	course	curriculum
	individual	group	
Duration – activity	50 minutes		
Intended learning outcome	Students are able to achieve team consensus on a proposal for interdisciplinary research; Students are able to synthesize insights from various points of view into a proposal for interdisciplinary research.		
Remarks			

Setup

a   Preparation teacher

Prepare a presentation with the instruction of the different steps and make an evaluation form for the pitches. Make interdisciplinary groups; students with different disciplinary backgrounds or expertise are put together in one group.

b   Preparation student

None.

c   Teaching setup

Step 1

Give a brief overview of the intended learning outcomes of this seminar. Then introduce the assignment by explaining that in 40 minutes a spaceship called 'The Interdisciplinary Shuttle' will depart for Kepler 62e. Kepler 62e is a planet that is quite similar to earth. It is full of life and harbours an intelligent civilization. Humanity would like to make contact with this intelligent species and learn everything about them. Yet, the planet is hard to access and it is impossible to communicate with earth once the shuttle has landed.

The capacity of the space shuttle is limited. There is room for only one interdisciplinary research team. The group that comes up with the best interdisciplinary research proposal in 40 minutes will be rewarded with an opportunity to conduct their research and be the first humans to study this alien civilization.

Step 2

Divide the students into groups of four people. Instruct the groups to pick a research topic 1) which every group member can work on based on their field of expertise and 2) is concise and narrowed down. After the teams have chosen their research topic the students have to answer the following questions:

a   What makes the topic appropriate to interdisciplinary inquiry?
b   Why is the topic relevant?
c   Is the topic specific enough?

The students have five minutes to choose their research topic and answer these three questions.

Step 3

During this step the students individually draw a mind map of their contribution to the research topic. Ask students to individually determine what they can contribute to the research, given their background, knowledge and skills. Instruct students to make a mind map of the theories, concepts and assumptions of their disciplinary perspective which they think are relevant for the research. Instruct the students to also include their disciplinary weakness in the mind map by answering the following questions:

1   What capacities do they lack considering the type of research?
2   What is their blind spot?

The students have only five minutes to finish this step.

Step 4

After the students have made their disciplinary mind maps, they have to find common ground between their disciplinary contributions in order to start working together. Instruct students to answer the following questions to bring the individual mind maps together:

1   Which contributions are most relevant for the research topic?
2   Can they discover connections/overlap between the individual contributions?
    Students have eight minutes to finish this step.

Step 5

Based on the analysis in the previous step, the teams can formulate a research question on their topic in five minutes. Instruct the students to formulate a precise, realistic and researchable question that makes use of the skills of all team members.

Step 6

During this step the students have to draft the methodology of the research they want to conduct in eight minutes. Explain to the students that they can conduct several disciplinary experiments or use an integrated method. Tell the students that there is no time for details.

Step 7

Explain that a pitch session will be held in order to choose the research team that will board the shuttle. The pitches will be evaluated according to the following three criteria:
1   Creativity: Is the research question and approach original?
2   Usefulness: Is the answer to the research question beneficial to science and/or society?
3   Interdisciplinarity: Does the research need an interdisciplinary approach? Does the team make use of the strengths of the disciplines of all its members?

Instruct the students to prepare a two-minute pitch that contains the research question, a justification for the methodology and a clear statement about how this approach is interdisciplinary. The students have five minutes to prepare for their pitch.

Step 8

Ask students to evaluate the pitches based on the three criteria mentioned in the previous step. You could hand out a form they could use (see assessment). Let every group pitch their research proposal. After the pitches explain how the voting will go. Every student can vote, but not for their own research.

d   Assessment

These forms can be used to assess the three criteria of creativity, usefulness and interdisciplinarity in the pitches.

The research question and approach are unclear and not original.	1	2	3	4	5	The research question and approach are very clear and original.

The answer to this research question does not have an added value for science nor society.	1	2	3	4	5	The answer to the research question will be very useful to science and/or society.

The question can be answered with only one discipline.	1	2	3	4	5	An interdisciplinary approach is needed to answer the question.
The team does not make use of the strengths of all the team members.	1	2	3	4	5	The team makes excellent use of the strengths of all the team members.

Example

During this activity, students with a background in sociology, anthropology and biology formulate the following research question:

To what extent does gender exist on Kepler e62?

Students with a background in biology, language studies and artificial intelligence formulate the following research question:

How can we communicate with inhabitants of Kepler e62?

Students with a background in economics, sociology, politics and mathematics formulate the following research question:

To what extent do market forces shape the society of Kepler e62?

Variations

To make this learning activity more appropriate for students with a lower level of interdisciplinary skills you expand the time limit of every step so it fits a two-hour tutorial. Expanding the time limit for students with a high level of interdisciplinary skills could result in a more in-depth proposal.

You could use Poll Everywhere as a tool for voting in step 8.

As an extension of the assignment, you can announce after the pitches that there is one more seat on the shuttle. The groups that are not going to Kepler 62e are asked to pitch which of their team members should fill this seat and complement the research team that is going to Kepler 62e. What disciplinary perspective is lacking in the winning team regarding the research they plan on the foreign planet? Have the winning team choose the extra research member after the pitches.

Another extension is to have students determine how their preliminary research question scores on the four defining criteria of a finalized research question. A finalized research question is (after Menken & Keestra, 2017):

1 Relevant: It should be related to the broader problem you wish to address, reflect the reason for your research project, and be the driver for interdisciplinary research. In short, it should be clear why it is worthwhile to seek an answer to the question.

2 Anchored: It should be the logical outcome of your literature review, expert interviews and theoretical framework. Your research question has to be embedded in the fields of knowledge of your research topic and the result should be of added value to the fields involved.
3 Researchable: It should be possible to conceive research methods that can address the question in the amount of time and with the means available.
4 Precise: It should be straightforward and specific. It should be clear what the research focus is.

To make sure that you reached the learning objectives of this assignment you could include a step 9 where you let the students reflect with their group on the process of formulating a common goal, and on the different biases that came up and how they dealt with them. You could then discuss this in a plenary session.

References

The framework of this ILA is derived from the curricular design within the Institute for Interdisciplinary Studies.

23 Managing data

Overview

Students learn how to collect and categorize information from different disciplinary perspectives in a shared document. This document gives an overview of the problems they encounter collectively and provides a basis for discussions.

Interdisciplinary skills	Ordering and structuring, analysing, a questioning attitude		
Characteristics	workshop	course	curriculum
	individual	group	
Duration – activity	90 minutes		
Intended learning outcome	Students are able to categorize information from literature of different disciplines in a data management table; Students can analyse the similarities, differences and conflicts between disciplines based on the information in the data management table.		
Remarks	You could hand out a data management table.		

Setup

a   Preparation teacher

You should have a clear assignment for the report including a deadline. Make an overview of the research teams and backgrounds of the team members. You can make the disciplinary teams before the first meeting.

b   Preparation student

The students work in a team of 3-4 students with different disciplinary backgrounds on an interdisciplinary research topic. The students have formulated a research question that they would like to study. The students have already searched for relevant articles from their disciplinary perspective that are related to a specific topic.

Teaching setup

Step 1

Introduce the data management table (DMT, see for an example page 97). Explain that a DMT is useful in interdisciplinary research because it is important to have a clear overview of the research related to the topic by making the different theories, concepts and assumptions explicit. Then explain how the table should be used and walk the students through the different columns (see example below).

Step 2

Let students individually fill in the DMT for their research topic. You can give them a handout of the DMT to fill in.

Step 3

Instruct the students to discuss their theories, concepts and assumptions with the research team and create one document with DMTs with the research group.

Tip: Make it a habit of rewarding students for their efforts and not only for their results, by saying 'good question', 'nice try' or 'interesting link you made'. This will stimulate students towards a growth mindset.

Step 4

Now that the students have a shared document with DMTs explain to them how they can be used to analyse the differences and conflicts between the disciplinary insights. Especially the conflicts create an opportunity for integration of the different insights. Once the students have established that there are differences, they should study the nature of these differences. The students can use the following questions to analyse the DMT:

1   Do the insights of different disciplines centre around the same topic about which they reveal different aspects?
2   Do some insights support each other? In what specific way do the disciplinary insights contradict or differ from each other? If disciplines use the same concept: how are these concepts defined and measured? Are assumptions in conflict? Are the differences a result of different research conditions?

Tip:
1   Using a wiki or googledocs may be useful for this learning activity, because students eventually have to share their information. Through this online software both teachers and students can create shared documents to work on jointly.
2   Epistemological assumptions are more hidden. You could suggest to students to browse through an introductory course book from the sub-discipline.
3   You can ask the students to use different colours for their individual contributions in the DMT.

Example

This is an example of a data management table where the different aspects of the table are explained (adapted from Menken & Keestra 2016).

Full reference to the book or article				
Discipline / sub-discipline	Theory / hypothesis	Concept(s)	Assumptions / methodology	Insight into problem
Name the specific research field and specialization.	Explain what it entails; describe the relation between the (f) actors that are considered or conjectured to be relevant (e.g. cause X and effects Y + Z, or the correlation between different (f)actors; or why a certain intervention is thought to be useful in helping to overcome the problem).	Analyse the key building blocks of the explanation or conceptualization captured in the theoretical framework. Give clear definitions of them. Explain which of the (potentially plural) definitions you will take as a point of departure in your research project.	Analyse the basic assumptions underlying your theoretical framework. Those assumptions can have an ontological, epistemological, methodological, or cultural philosophical nature, i.e. they can be related to our views on reality, and to our views on how we can gain knowledge about that reality, how we can best study that reality, and about how science can contribute to society. Explain which assumptions you will incorporate, or which you reject.	Explain how the theory and the key concepts it entails help to provide more insight in or a possible solution to the problem you are addressing. Also take into consideration possible limitations.

Variations

You can incorporate this DMT in an interdisciplinary research project.

Between step 2 and 3 you can let the students discuss the relevant theories, concepts and assumptions with fellow students with a similar disciplinary background.

If students are not familiar with searching for academic resources you could discuss with them how to find information efficiently and how to check the quality of resources. For example, explain that reading relevant review articles first will help them to recognize the main theories. Online information about the author can also be helpful for this step.

If students are not accustomed to critically analysing texts, you can use one article as an example. Every student should read this article before the lecture, and hand in a completed DMT as a homework assignment. During the seminar you can discuss the students' findings, answer questions and address any problems they encountered. The mini-guide Critical Thinking (Paul & Elder, 2009) provides handy tools for a critical analysis of texts.

You could encourage students to ask experts in the field about the concepts, theories and assumptions they encounter.

If you want to include an assessment you could let the students write a short group report (about the differences and the overlap they have identified between the theories, concepts and assumptions. This assignment stimulates the students to meet outside class to discuss the DMT in more detail. In this way students experience that communication is essential in interdisciplinary research. You can provide feedback to the students.

References

This ILA is part of *An Introduction to Interdisciplinary Research: Theory and Practice* by S. Menken & M. Keestra (2016).

The framework of this ILA is derived from the curricular design within the Association for Integrative Studies.

The example of this ILA was developed by teachers of Interdisciplinary Social Sciences (ASW) at the University of Amsterdam.

  ○ Boix Mansilla, V., Dawes Duraisingh, E., Wolfe, C.R., & Haynes, C. (2009a). Targeted Assessment Rubric: An Empirically Grounded Rubric for Interdisciplinary Writing, *The Journal of Higher Education*, 80(3), 334-353.
  ○ Calhoun, C., (2012). *Classical and Contemporary Sociological Theory Readers*, John Wiley & Sons Inc.: Hoboken, New Jersey.

24 Inter-professional team meeting

Overview

Students are appointed different professional roles in a real or fictitious case and learn to formulate a common goal or solution. Students learn to work together with peers who have different perspectives on the topic at hand and who are related to different professional roles in a project.

Interdisciplinary skills	Formulating a common goal, shared leadership, reflection		
Characteristics	workshop	course	curriculum
	individual	group	
Duration - activity	120 minutes		
Intended learning outcome	Students are able to achieve team consensus on a goal or solution that exceeds individual stakes; Students are able to use the P.I.N. method to reflect on and evaluate the collaboration in the team, including the group atmosphere, leadership and the interactions between team members.		
Remarks			

Setup

a   Preparation teacher

Choose a topic for an inter-professional case. This can be a complex problem of a client either inside or outside academia. The case has to contain at least four actors of different disciplines, who are able to offer different solutions to the problem. Divide the students into groups, so that every group has the same number of students as the number of actors from the case. Then assign one student to be the chair and one to be the secretary next to their role of an actor. Provide the students with an agenda of the meeting. Preferably, you read the solution of the different actors before the actual meeting.

Tip: This activity works best if it is a real-life case, as it increases students' motivation to work on solutions that may be put into practice by a client.

b   Preparation student
Read the instructions given about the inter-professional team meeting. Write a concept solution for the inter-professional case ahead of the team meeting by analysing the case from your own disciplinary view. Write down the contributions, needs and possible motives of your professional role. Based on this analysis you formulate possible interventions or actions suited to the formulated solution.

c   Teaching setup
Step 1
Welcome the students to the inter-professional meeting. Explain that one student is the chair and one the secretary and briefly explain their tasks. They will keep this role during the analysis of the case and the formulation of the common goal or solution. Explain that during the meeting you will be only observing their interaction and that you will chair the evaluation afterwards.
Have an introduction round in which students introduce themselves and their disciplines.

Tip: If the students don't know each other let them make name cards and have them write their disciplinary background on this card as well.

Step 2
Let the chair take the lead during the meeting following the provided agenda and instruction. You can support the chair if necessary when it comes to time management and the equal contribution of all actors. Ask more in-depth questions about the feasibility of their solution.

Step 3
Let the students reflect on their collaboration after the meeting, regarding the group atmosphere, interactions, group standards and leadership.
Use the P.I.N. (positive, interesting, negative) method to support the reflection. Ask each student to write down a positive, interesting and negative experience concerning the collaboration, including how s/he feels about it. Give students approximately five minutes to do this.
Lead this discussion to stimulate reflective thinking by asking reflective questions. Relate questions to specific situations that were observed during the meeting. Additionally, use the following questions to stimulate a reflective response and discussion:

Group atmosphere
- How was the group atmosphere (cosy, a battle, a flight, dependence, quarrelsome?)
- Did everyone participate actively in the discussion of the case and did everyone give his or her opinion or advice?
- Were there any tensions in the team?
- Was it possible to give feedback on both the process and the content of the team meeting?

Interactions
- Were there any issues between team members?
- Were the interactions between members personal or pragmatic?
- Was there a kind of rivalry?
- Did any subgroup emerge within the team during the meeting?

Leadership
- What kind of leadership could be observed during the meeting?
- How would you define the style of leadership?
- Did differences in power between team members play a noticeable role?
- Was anyone overbearing during the meeting?

d   Assessment
The care plan can be assessed using the following rubric:
- The competence of the medical expert and co-worker are the most important competences for this assignment;
- If the medical expert and/or collaborator is 'below expectations' according to the criteria below, the overall judgment is also 'below expectation';
- If the medical expert and collaborator are 'above expectations' according to the following criteria, and the remaining competences are minimally 'as expected' then the overall judgment is also 'above expectations';
- In all other cases, the final judgment is 'as expected'.

Competence	Below expectation	According to expectations	Above expectations
Medical expert	Patient's history is incomplete; Publication years are not listed; Incorrect indication of medication; Insufficient evidence of somatic suffering and the resulting disorders and limitations.	Relevant history of patient has been mentioned; Publication years are listed; Medical terminology is used; Right or left handed is mentioned; Medication is reported in generic names and correct dosage and administration forms; There are indications of insight into somatic suffering and the resulting disorders and limitations.	According to expectations, whereby the following aspects are provided as well: insight into the prognosis of the conditions and consequences for the future, are provided.
Collaborator	No personal goals of the patient have been formulated and/or there is no attention for the involvement of paramedics; The reflection report of the group meeting of the students at Zuyd University is missing.	The care plan shows that the patient's goals have been drawn up together with the patient, taking into account his or her wishes and quality of life; Considerations are given about the involvement of paramedics; The group reflection report of the meeting with the students of Zuyd is present as well as the individual reflection on the process.	According to expectations, whereby the following aspects are provided as well: the plans shows signs of talking to the patient's family, it appears that the student is aware of the professional field of paramedics and the way in which they can contribute (specifically) to the achievement of the goals

▼

Organizer	The care plan has not been put to the discussion board and/or not sent to Zuyd Hogeschool on time; Formulated goals are not realistic.	The care plan has been put on the discussion board and sent to Zuyd Hogeschool on time; Formulated goals are realistic and there has been thought about funding.	According to expectations, whereby the following aspect is provided as well: clear knowledge of the financing structure of health care.
Health promotor	There is insufficient attention for influential and non-influential risky determinants of health and insufficient attention to contextual factors that may affect the patient's situation; The ICF model is not applied; No measurement instrument was used to determine the 'vulnerability'.	Attention has been paid to influential and non-influential risky determinants of health and to contextual factors that may affect the patient's situation; The ICF model is applied; A measuring instrument has been used to determine the 'vulnerability'.	According to expectations, whereby the following aspect is provided as well: influential and non-influential risky determinants are part of the care plan. Plan of action is described. Multiple measuring instruments have been used to determine the vulnerability.
Professional practitioner	The care plan is not an objective representation of the situation; The patient's dependent position is not taken into account; The limits on privacy are clearly not respected.	The care plan is an objective representation of the situation; The care plan shows respect for interpersonal differences; and takes into account the patient's dependent position.	According to expectations, whereby the following aspect is provided as well: Cultural differences are taken into account; Ethical dilemmas are clearly described and possibly supported by literature; The limits on the privacy of the patient are respected where they fall outside the scope of health assistance.

Example

Students simulate an authentic inter-professional team meeting in which the clients' goals and health (care) demands are the starting point.

A team meeting consisted of approximately five medical students from Maastricht University, five students from Zuyd University of Applied Sciences who follow the educational programmes: Arts Therapies, Occupational Therapy, Speech and Language Therapy, Physiotherapy and Nursing at the Faculty of Healthcare and one student from Gilde Education, who follows the vocational programme of Nursing. Each of the fifth-year medical students chose a real-life case addressing a frail elder client from their primary care placement. Before each meeting, information about the frail elder client (anamnesis and personal goals) was provided to the students from Zuyd University of Applied Sciences and the students from Gilde Education. Based on their specific discipline, all students prepared a care plan for each client case using the International Classification of Functioning framework (World Health Organization, 2001) and Dutch guidelines if possible.

The care plans were then discussed during the inter-professional team meeting and all the discipline-specific care plans were integrated into a single inter-professional care plan for each case. In this inter-professional team meeting the students first formulated a common description of the client's situation by answering the following questions: What is the client's situation and the client's relatives' situation? Do we have a complete picture of the client's situation? Then the team decided which client goal they were going to focus on. When the goal was agreed upon, students analysed what the client, relatives of the client and the team needed to realize this goal. Based on this analysis the students formulated a proposal with an overview of the specific actions that needed to be taken in order to achieve the goal. Next, students formulated specific plans of action where responsibilities were settled. In this phase it was important that students decided on who could contribute to these actions starting with the client and the clients' relatives. Lastly the team evaluated whether the care plan met the client's goal. The figure below provides a visual overview of the previously described step-by-step plan to discuss clients collaboratively (van Dongen, under review).

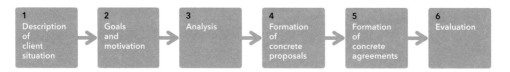

After the team meeting, the students reflected on the assignment and their collaboration, including the group atmosphere, their interactions with each other, group standards and leadership. Lecturers acted as facilitators during the process of the inter-professional team meeting and as supervisors overseeing the reflection process.

Variations

You can use this workshop to start a project.

To increase the level for the chair and secretary you could let them make an agenda for the meeting and invite the other actors.

Give the students secret motives attached to their role. For example, role A does not want to cooperate immediately with role B. These motives run parallel to the motives of other roles. The students are not allowed to directly reveal their motives, but they do have to try to incorporate these motives in the final solution.

You could add a step 4 where the different teams present their integrated solution.

References

The framework of this activity is developed by Albine Moser, Hester Smeets, Jerome van Dongen, Marion van Lierop and Miriam Janssen from Zuyd University of Applied Sciences and Maastricht University.

The example of this inter-professional team meeting is from Zuyd University of Applied Sciences, Faculty of Health in collaboration with Maastricht University, Faculty of Medicine. The educational material comes from the RAAK Pro project 'Inter-professional self-management support for clients with chronic diseases in primary care. Content and collaboration concerning tailored goal setting'.

Factsheets inter-professional education from Zuyd University of Applied Sciences: www.zuyd.nl/onderzoek/lectoraten/autonomie-en-participatie/onderwijs-en-professionalisering/interprofessioneel-opleiden-en-samenwerken

- World Health Organization (2010). *Framework for Action on Interprofessional Education & Collaborative Practice*. Geneva: World Health Organization.
- World Health Organization (2001). *International class cation of functioning, disabilities and health problems*. Geneva: World Health Organization.
- Dongen J.J. van, Bokhoven M.A. van, Goossens W.N.M., Daniëls R., Weijden T. van der, Beurskens A. (Under review). Development of a customizable programme for improving interprofessional team meetings. An action research approach. *International Journal of Integrated Care*.

Courses

25 Scenario analysis

Overview

Students learn to analyse, integrate and present trends and facts that interact in complex ways by using scenario analysis. This method consists of several steps, and focuses on the future.

Interdisciplinary skills	Sound decision making, situation awareness, analysing		
Characteristics	workshop	course	curriculum
	individual	group	
Duration - activity	150 minutes		
Intended learning outcome	Students are able to anticipate at least one plausible outcome of a complex problem while using a scenario analysis method.		
Remarks	You could either do this ILA in one long workshop or divide the ILA into different parts during the course.		

Setup

a   Preparation teacher

Optional: Prepare specific topics you'd like the students to explore during this learning activity.

This learning activity involves several exercises within one method (the scenario analysis). The success of this ILA largely depends on the level of motivation of the students and the timing of this activity within the course. This demands adequate and realistic planning when students will hand in their assignments and when they receive feedback (communicate deadlines to students, be sure they have enough time for the different elements of the ILA).

b   Teaching setup

Step 1 (15 minutes)

Divide the students into groups of 3-5 students. Within their group, they decide on a topic they want to explore. If your course has specific topics, you can use these topics for this activity.

Step 2: Brainstorming about the future
(depending on the variation, at least 45 minutes)

The first task for the students is to think creatively about possible futures for the chosen topic. At this stage, it is important to tell students that anything is possible; there are no boundaries and the students are encouraged to think outside the box. Various methods can be used to achieve this (see variations).

Step 3: Analysing trends (at least 30-45 minutes)

The next step is to ask students to analyse and structure the ideas generated in step 1. In this step, students search for academic and non-academic literature to support the trends. These trends should reflect a wide variety of information and include different domains, such as the political, the socioeconomical, the cultural, the ecological and the technical domain.

Optional: Let the students do the literature search at home and start the next lecture with step 4.

Step 4: Formulating the driving forces of the future (10 minutes)

Based on the gathered information, students select two driving forces which will have a great impact on the future of their chosen topic, but of which the outcomes are still uncertain and hard to predict.

Step 5: Drawing a scenario framework (20 minutes)

Ask the students to draw the scenario framework, based on two axes. The driving forces are the axes of a scenario framework. In this way, four possible futures are mapped. The axes are continuums and the ends of each axis represent the most extreme outcomes. The students pick one scenario for further analysis. They may choose a best-case or a worst-case scenario.

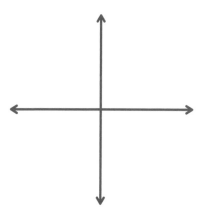

In the final stage, students take their scenario as a starting point from which they work back towards the present by identifying steps that need to be taken, and anticipating things that need to happen to realize their future scenario. Once they have developed a coherent timeline, they present their scenario through storytelling. This means that the students will describe all different steps from now until their future scenario into one coherent story. A story enables the students to present the complex interplay of causal relationships.

Example

Since this ILA is complicated and consists of many steps, the following example is a description of the interpretation of the scenario analysis by a group of students. This example can help you to understand the method of the scenario analysis and the steps that need to be taken by the students.

Scenarios of the future of agriculture

Step 1

In the 'Sustainable Dynamics' course, a group of four first-year students in Future Planet Studies decided to explore the future of agriculture. In their first brainstorm session about possible future trends within this theme, they thought of genetically modified products, food conflicts and wars as a result of a worldwide food crisis, the exchange of knowledge on extensive land use, changing norms and values concerning food, urban farming and, lastly, the end of hunger.

Step 2

By analysing these ideas and trends, they found that there was uncertainty about methods of land use: trends were pointing in the direction of both more intensive and more extensive land use. The pattern of globalization concerning food was also an important but uncertain factor.

Step 3

The students formulated technology and innovation as the driving forces behind the development of type of land use, and economic ethics as the key driving force behind the development towards either more globalization or more protectionism.

Step 4
Their scenario framework looked like this:

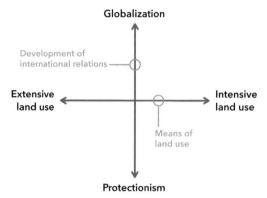

The desirable future of extensive land use and international cooperation was chosen for further analysis. Through retrospective research, the students found that a transition in thinking about land use, diet and international aid was needed to meet the conditions of this scenario. Although less desirable, the awareness and readiness for action would be triggered by a worldwide food crisis as a result of overexploitation and market competition.

Variations

There are several ways to stimulate creative thinking:

- The Walt Disney strategy (see page 71).
- Ask students to write an essay as a homework assignment in the form of a diary of a student in the year 2060. The essay should cover one day in the life of this student and should be about their chosen topic. Below is an extract from the essay written by one of the students in the group that focused on agriculture:
  It's 7 o'clock and I didn't sleep at all last night, thanks to the genetically modified glow in the dark fish that I got as a present. Unfortunately, I have to get up now since we're going on an excursion to the Museum for Agriculture. It's the only place in the Netherlands where they still apply intensive agricultural land use. It's become part of our cultural heritage, since intensive land use led to severe soil degradation and food insecurity. I've heard we're even allowed to taste some products, which is exciting, since I've never tasted 'authentic vegetables' or 'traditional meat'. They say it tastes better, but obviously in-vitro meat is much more nutritious and healthier.
- A story or film script is a way to present a future scenario to academic or non-academic audiences. The following points of interest for storytelling will make the future reality more plausible and imaginable: think of a catchy name, make use of metaphors, pay attention to details and integrate both current 'certain' and possible future trends.

References

The framework of this ILA is derived from the curricular design within the Institute for Interdisciplinary Studies.

26 Managing teamwork in big groups

Overview

This interdisciplinary learning activity focuses on cooperation within a group where there is tension between students who contribute to the group project and those who do not ('freeriding') by creating dilemma's.

Interdisciplinary skills	Situation awareness, formulating a common goal, reflection		
Characteristics	workshop	course	curriculum
	individual	group	
Duration – activity	Two-hour classes twice per week for seven weeks		
Intended learning outcome	Students are able to use surveys to reflect on their cooperation in the group; Students are able to recognize and deal with freeriders to achieve project results.		
Remarks			

Setup

a   Preparation teacher

Prepare a group project assignment in which students tackle a problem, like setting up a business or the management of a common resource. Let students choose their topic for the project. This induces students' ownership and motivation. Divide the students randomly into groups of more than eight students.

b   Preparation student

None.

c   Teaching setup

Step 1

Introduce the group assignment in the first week of the course. Explain that you will assess students on individual work but that their peers will also assess them for their contributions to the group's project. During the second week, students continue to work on the group assignment.

Step 2

In week three of the course send out the online Progress survey #1, which focuses on the question: How could you or other members improve the teamwork? This qualitative assessment forces the students to stop and reflect on the dynamics in the team. Include a quantitative part and ask the students to allocate 100% among other group members, with higher percentages going to team members who contribute more and lower percentages going to those who contribute less (freeride). Discuss the anonymized results of the first progress survey with the entire class, so that each group can also learn from the feedback of other groups.

Step 3

In week four introduce the quiz, which is meant to make them aware of their interdependence of each other and to push them to think even further about their fellow students in terms of trust, dependency and asymmetric information. Explain that the quiz involves a simple question including the following explanation:

Another student will get an A if you get this question right but an
F if you get it wrong. You will receive an A or not, depending on
how another student answers this same question. You are not paired
with another student in the sense that their decision affects you or
vice versa.
What is 1+1?

The trick is to match each student with another student anonymously. This way of matching removes the potential thought of a reciprocal game and introduces the entire group as a 'partner'. Getting the right answer to the simple question gives the answering student an A but their partner a B whereas getting it wrong means the answering student gets a B but the other student gets an A except that both students get Cs (rather than As) if they both answer it right. This activity can also be run with a 'cheap-talk' component in which students can talk about their strategies aloud even as they answer in secret. This quiz can motivate a class discussion on risk, communication, trust, repeated games etc. and their effects on cooperation.

Step 4

In week five swap a significant (40%) randomly chosen minority of students with another team to test the team's cohesion by disrupting their tacit knowledge and institutions. Do this without warning the students. This swap will force all students to rearrange themselves, redefine roles and tasks and introduce their new members to the informal institutions the group has already created. The students will finish the group assignment with their new team. To build trust between the team members do a team-building exercise that suits the group of students (see tips for examples).

Tip: Practice 'trust falls' with the group to build trust between the team members. A trust fall is a group exercise in which a person deliberately allows him/herself to fall, relying on the other members of the group to catch him/her.

Tip: To build trust between team members, ask each team to make the 'ultimate team member' by combining each team member's strengths and positive attributes into one imaginary person. This 'person' should also receive a name, have his/her picture drawn and his/her different attributes labelled. The teams should also write a story about this person, highlighting all the things their imaginary person can do with all of their amazing characteristics. At the end of the exercise each team should share their person with the group.

Step 5
Send out Progress survey #2 in week six, which focuses again on the question how you and your other team members could improve the team's work. Students continue working on the group assignment.

Step 6
Students give an in-class presentation in week seven. The feedback they receive is used to improve their group report on the assignment.

Step 7
In week eight (the last week of the course), the students hand in the final report and then fill in Progress survey #3 including the following questions:
1 What was the best part of your project and teamwork?
2 What would you have done differently, if you had to do it again with new random partners?
3 What lessons have you learned that you would apply to future team projects?

In addition, they should allocate 100% among their teammates again.

d   Assessment

Besides their grade for the group project, students are assessed on individual assignments of the instructor's choice, e.g., homework assignments, individual presentation, participation in class discussions, etc.

The students are also assessed on their individual contribution to a group presentation (20% of the course grade) and their individual contribution to the group report (30% of the course grade). This assessment begins with a base grade on each item that is then adjusted up/down according to the results from the three progress surveys, with weights of 1/6, 1/3 and 1/2 on the first, second and third surveys to put more weight on later surveys which are more likely to reflect students' understanding of each other.

The adjustment up/down can be as much as one grade up or down, e.g. from a base grade of 85% down to a 75% for a 'free-rider' or up to a 95% for a 'helpful' teammate. The net adjustment is zero across all students.

The actual drop can be calculated in several ways (using standard deviations or just a ratio). The simplest way to do this is to adjust the largest up/down grade by 10% and then use that point to calibrate the (absolute value) of the adjustment to other grades.

Example

Example of the assessment rating

Students are divided into groups of nine. Average weights were 12.5% each (students omit themselves). If Alice got an average of 10% on progress 1 from her eight peers, 8% on progress 2 and 12% on progress 3, for a weighted average of 10.33%. If Barbara gets 15%, 17% and 20%, then that's an average of 18.17%. Assume Barbara is farthest from 12.5%.

Assuming the group grade is 84%, then Barbara will get a 94% and Alice will get 80%. That 80% is found by taking the difference between the mean (12.5%) and the most extreme score (Barbara's 18.17%) and dividing that number (5.67) into 10% to get 1.76 – the 'adjustment factor' that is then multiplied by each student's difference from 12.5%. For Alice this is 2.17%, which gives a grade of 84% – (2.17%*1.76) = 80.17%.

The grades for swapped students are pro-rated 50/50 between their old/new group for both the presentation and group report.

Tip: Although these adjustments are complex to describe, they are fairly easy to programme in a spreadsheet but double-check your work!

Variations

This activity was originally designed as a project where a large group of students tackled a common pool resource problem, while at the same time experiencing the same group dynamics in their teamwork as users of the common pool Resource experience while sharing (usually overexploiting or underproviding) the common-pool resource. The theoretical content about group dynamics in common pool resources of this learning activity can be found in Zetland (2017).

References

○ Zetland, D. Teaching Common-Pool Resource Management (July 5, 2017). Available at SSRN: https://ssrn.com/abstract=2906697

27 Developing a campaign

Overview

Students learn to develop a media strategy based on a thorough academic analysis of a solution to a complex problem. The students analyse the potential of an actual solution proposed by an actor in the field and develop a media campaign for their own solution.

Interdisciplinary skills	Sound decision making, evaluating and analysing		
Characteristics	workshop	course	curriculum
	individual	group	
Duration – activity	Eight weeks		
Intended learning outcome	Students are able to integrate knowledge and expertise from different disciplines in a solution; Students are able to present their solution in a media strategy.		
Remarks			

Setup

a   Preparation teacher

Put the assignment on an online platform at the start of the course. In the first week you have to organize two lectures on a specific topic. The students perform the various steps in this assignment by themselves.
Divide the students into groups of 3-4 students. The students have to attend these lectures. Organize a symposium where the different campaigns are presented.

b   Preparation student

None.

c   Teaching setup

Step 1 (week 1)

Give two lectures about a complex problem that requires an interdisciplinary approach to find a solution. After the two lectures, instruct the students to hand in an introduction and problem statement, including:

1 A problem statement based on academic literature.
2 A short analysis of the proposed solution.

Step 2 (week 2)

Now the problem statement is clear, the students have to write a short theoretical text which includes an analysis of the problem. Ask students to define the core concepts with regard to the chosen theme and ask them to write a theoretical section about the background of these concepts by searching and reading a selection of relevant scientific literature. The group members should make a selection and read relevant literature about the chosen topic. They need to include at least six academic articles. The students should answer the following questions: What knowledge does this article add to our academic analysis.

Step 3 (week 3)

The students work on a thorough academic analysis of the problem and start developing a solution to the problem based on the academic analysis.

Step 4 (week 4)

The students work on a thorough academic analysis of the problem and hand in their analysis including a proposed solution at the end of the week.

Step 5 (week 5)

The next step is to translate this solution based on an academic analysis in more practical terms. The students have to develop a media strategy, by answering the following questions: What is the goal of the media product? Should it be to raise awareness, is it meant to be inspiring, compelling, a call to action or is the intention to change existing behavioural patterns? Which media and campaign form is most suitable to reach your goal? What is your target group and why? Let the students explain their choices.

Step 6 (week 6)

Ask the students to put their idea developed in the previous into practice, by working on the final media product itself.

Step 7 (week 7)

Let the students work on the media product.

Step 8 (week 8)

Let the students hand in the report including their campaign product and instruct the groups to give a presentation about their campaign during the symposium.

The future of food

In the first week, an introductory lecture was given to explain the assignment and to feed the students some ideas about possible pathways towards solving the world food issue, for example starting a media campaign, lobbying or writing a strategic policy recommendation.

In the subsequent meetings, stakeholders from the field presented various examples to trigger students' imagination, inspire them and enhance their creativity.

One of the stakeholders was the Royal Tropical Institute (KIT). Its representative talked about challenges in food-production systems. Agriculture is fundamental to promote sustainable economic development and the key for KIT is the perspective of the smallholder/small-scale farmer.

The goal of KIT is to assist smallholders/small-scale farmers to improve their livelihoods through entrepreneurship/access to markets, and food security.

Value chain development is a key concept in strategies to reduce rural poverty in developing countries. The basic idea is that value chains offer farmers (and indeed all chain actors) the opportunity to acquire new knowledge from actors elsewhere in the chain.

Another stakeholder who participated in the discussion was a representative of the Youth Food Movement (YFM), which is committed to promoting a fairer and healthier food system. Through events such as eat-ins, debates, the Food Film Festival and the YFM Academy, the movement endeavours to make people aware of the food choices they make.

In consultation with the lecturer, the students subsequently picked a theme to work on, decided on the form of the end product, formed a group together with other students and started working on the assignment. The students can work on, for example: creating a video documentary, designing a new and innovative value chain structure, creating a petition, writing a speech or strategic policy advice for the EU Committee or another (inter)national organization or sending in a tender for an important (inter)national scientific institution.

One of the groups from the Future of Food project designed the 'WeCantWaste Challenge': During one weekend participants had to live from food that otherwise would have been wasted. The students wanted to contribute towards a renewed appreciation of our food and stimulate behavioural change. They had articles placed in different newspaper and organized an online campaign.

Variations

You can include pitches where the students explain the what, why and how of their campaign. The group can give feedback on this.

You can include extra tutorials in the course setup. Students can discuss their progress with you, and receive feedback on the preliminary results they hand in.

In step 4 you could stimulate students to reflect on their own contribution to the team as well. Let the students score themselves in process-related criteria, such as listening skills, the ability to meet deadlines, conflict management and input in team meetings, etc.

To stimulate discussion about the group process, incorporate instruments such as the Belbin team role questionnaire.

References

The framework of this ILA is derived from the curricular design within the Institute for Interdisciplinary Studies.

28 Stakeholder's view

Overview

Students experience a stakeholder dialogue in a case with conflicting interests by taking the perspective of one of the stakeholders. In the preparation for the dialogue, students learn to analyse the motives of different stakeholders, understand them and how they can best respond to these different motives.

Interdisciplinary skills	Analysing, perspective taking, sound decision making		
Characteristics	workshop	course	curriculum
	individual	group	
Duration – activity	Two times 90-120 minutes		
Intended learning outcome	Students are able to argue about a problem from a stakeholder's perspective; Students are able to present a stakeholder's perspective regarding this problem.		
Remarks			

Setup

a   Preparation teacher

Prepare a case with conflicting interests between different stakeholders involved in a project or resource. This can be a fictional as well as an empirical case (i.e. sand and gravel extraction in the Waddenzee). Make sure that the case has 4-5 different stakeholders.

Prepare some literature that the students can look over to prepare for the first tutorial.

Divide the students into groups of 10-12 students. Each group of students will have a dialogue about the prepared case.

b   Preparation student
The students read the case literature to prepare for the first tutorial.

c   Teaching setup
Step 1
Explain the assignment. Tell the students that they will be holding a meeting in three weeks' time in order to make agreements about how to solve the problem at stake or how a particular resource should be used.
After you have explained the assignment, start analysing the issue together with the students by writing down the different issues and actors on the blackboard. Next, ask the students to assign the roles of specific stakeholders. Two students represent every single stakeholder. Two students are appointed as the chairs, and their role is to organize and chair the meeting in an objective way.
Instruct the students to write a position paper (3,000 words) about their stakeholder's position and vision regarding the problem or resource. In order to write a proper position paper, students have to conduct a small literature study. The chairs write a report about the meeting instead of a position paper.

Step 2
Instruct the chairs to collect the position papers of the stakeholders and organize a meeting to discuss how the problem should be solved or how the resource should be used. The goal of the meeting is to gain a better understanding of the perspectives of the stakeholders and to search for a solution in a constructive manner. The chairs prepare an agenda based on the position papers they received from the different stakeholders. The meeting will take approximately two hours.

Step 3
During the meeting the teacher assesses the group process. The chairs are in charge of the meeting.

d   Assessment

The following rubric can be used to assess the quality of the meeting.

1. Argumentation

	1	2	3	4	5

- Does the attitude and argumentation reflect the attitude and argumentation of the stakeholder/chair in reality?
- Do the stakeholders use relevant arguments?
- Do the stakeholders use a variety of arguments?
- Are the allegations controllable and supported by examples and facts?
- Do the conclusions follow logically from the argumentation?
- Do the arguments correspond with the arguments presented in the position paper?
- Are arguments presented by other stakeholders addressed?
- Is the overall argument clear and consistent?
- Are the arguments original?

2. Presentation

	1	2	3	4	5

- Verbal communication: clarity, word choice and language (eloquence), conciseness, humour.
- Non-verbal communication: posture, eye/ facial expressions, gestures, eye contact.
- Verbal communication: articulation, volume, tempo, intonation, rest/dynamics, telling/not reading.
- Other points in the presentation: time use, structure, joining the other speakers.

3. Strategy

	1	2	3	4	5

- Are arguments introduced at the right moment in the dialogue (timing)?
- Are the chairs and other stakeholders played in a smart way? (This has to do with timing, but also ethos, pathos, in short with rhetoric).
- Are the questions and objections addressed to the other parties powerful?
- Do the participants really listen to each other and are they trying to establish a dialogue?
- Are concrete suggestions presented or proposals formulated to build bridges between the different positions of the stakeholders?

4. Teamwork

	1	2	3	4	5

- Do the stakeholders operate as a team?
- Is there a balance in speaking? Does every stakeholder get the same amount of time to speak?

Example

'Policy and Practice Role Play'

In the course The Politics of Education, Conflict and International Development, master students of the research master International Development Studies simulate a consultation meeting in Myanmar with key stakeholders. Creating a direct connection to policy and practice, students work with the Conflict Sensitive Education Pack (www.ineesite.org/en/conflict-sensitive-education), which is developed by the International Network for Education in Emergencies (INEE).

This simulation resembles an actual real-life situation about the implementation of Myanmar's education reform programme in the conflict-affected context of Myanmar. The goal of the educational reform in Myanmar is to modernize the education system for Myanmar's integration into ASEAN and the global economy and to improve access to quality education. Next to this, education plays an important role in the peace dialogue between the government and multiple ethnic armed groups. The simulated consultation round is about the design of conflict-sensitive education programming, and small groups of (2-3) students represent a wide range of international and local stakeholders (including the National Ministry of Education, Myanmar Education Consortium, Monastic Education Development Group, UNICEF, JICA, All Burma federation of student unions, Pa-oh Youth group, the GEN [gender equality network]).

Preparations

- Students are requested to read all relevant material provided, and in addition to explore the work of the actor they represent.
- Students prepare a three-minute pitch (and accompanying visual support in the form of a presentation or poster) to introduce their actor before the start of the role play (brief history/introduction of actor, main mission, main strategy).
- Students prepare their actor's strategy for the debate by handing in a short (two-page) overview of key debating points, overview of strategic allies and possible opposing actors, and an overview of desired outcomes of the debate.

Assessment

Students are assessed by a combination of two lecturers, and a guest from policy/practice, all using a grading sheet which focuses on the content and resources for the actor pitch (max. three points); presentation skills (max. two points); and active participation/line of argumentation (max. five points).

Variations

Feedback on the draft position paper could be incorporated.

Students could write a short statement that the chair will publish before the meeting, so that the students know the starting position of the other stakeholders.

If the students have little experience chairing a meeting, this could be trained in a separate tutorial.

To include some form of giving feedback and reflection, students could watch another stakeholder meeting and reflect on this process by for example using the grading form as a guideline.

Let the chairs act as stakeholders as well to make it more challenging for excellent students, because they have two different interests at the same time.

References

The framework of this ILA is derived from the curricular design within the Institute for Interdisciplinary Studies and the role-play example is developed by Dr Mieke Lopes Cardozo, from the research master International Development Studies.

29 Movies & matter

Overview

Small groups of students make connections between different disciplinary concepts that were addressed during lectures in a course. Students learn to visualize and connect these concepts and to present them to a public through the use of film.

Interdisciplinary skills	Formulating a common goal, analysing, reasoning		
Characteristics	workshop	course	curriculum
	individual	group	
Duration – activity	90 minutes		
Intended learning outcome	Students are able to explain and visualize the connections between three different concepts in max. five minutes of film.		
Remarks	You need a camera for each group of 4-5 students.		

Setup

a   Preparation teacher

Make a handout of the concepts that have been addressed in previous classes during the course. You could order the concepts according to the disciplines in which the concepts have been used.

Make a homework assignment that clearly states the goal of this activity, what the deadline is and how it will be assessed. Create a shared channel for uploading the film clips.

b   Preparation student

The students must have attended the previous classes.

c   Teaching setup
     Step 1
     Explain the goal of the assignment. The students have to produce a film clip of 2-5 minutes about the three concepts that have been addressed during the course. The clip should explain what the three concepts are, how they are interrelated, what the missing links are (optional) and what is still unknown about these concepts (optional). After the explanation, divide the students into groups of 4-5.

     Step 2
     Give the students the handout with a pool of concepts. Each group of students picks three concepts (one from each column) based on their own interests.

     Step 3
     Instruct the students to make a film script for a film of 2-5 minutes. The script forms the basis for the film. The students should make use of and refer to the literature and researchers that have played an important role in the general understanding of these concepts.

     Tip: If your students are not (yet) accustomed to connecting different disciplinary concepts you could include a feedback moment in the script or storyboard. Giving feedback will ensure that the end product is of minimum quality.

     Step 4
     Instruct the students to produce the clip based on the script as a homework assignment. Give students approximately three weeks to make the video clip. They are free to produce their films the way they prefer, but encourage them not to simply copy and paste video material from the internet. Tell students that they should upload their films onto a shared channel.

     Tip: Provide clear expectations for students. This could include assessment criteria or examples of completed movies from previous courses. Especially for undergraduate students this is useful, based on the criteria or examples they can draw up a list of tasks and assign personal responsibilities, tasks and deadlines. This is an informal collaboration contract.

d   Assessment
     You could use this rubric to assess the video clip. The different criteria correspond to the interdisciplinary skills

Criteria	Level 1	Level 2	Level 3	Level 4
Reasoning	Incorrect explanation of the three different concepts	Correct explanation of the three different concepts	Correct explanation of the three different concepts and incorporation of new information based on not more than three papers.	Correct explanation of the three different concepts and incorporation of new information based on more than three papers.
Analysing	The three different concepts are not connected.	Two of the three concepts are correctly connected.	All three concepts are correctly connected.	All three concepts are correctly connected and one new or original link is correctly added.
Formulating a common goal	The video clip has no main message. Missing links and what is still unknown is not shown.	The video clip has an unclear main message. Missing links and what is still unknown is not shown.	The video clip has a clear main message. Missing links and what is still unknown is not shown.	The video clip has a clear main message Missing links and what is still unknown is addressed.
Creativity	The clip shows creativity in one of the following aspects: decor, visuals, design and scenarios.	The clip shows creativity in two of the following aspects: decor, visuals, design and scenarios.	The clip shows creativity in three of the following aspects: decor, visuals, design and scenarios.	The clip shows creativity in all aspects: decor, visuals, design and scenarios.

Example

List of concepts of natural & social-science-based matter

The following list of concepts can be used if this learning activity is related to natural-science-based courses:

Physics	Biology	Chemistry
Cosmic microwave background	Mitogen activated protein (MAP) kinase pathway	Proteins
Deuterium	Cell membrane and the intake of substrates	Water
Entropy	Human anatomy	Conformation
Galaxy	Golgi apparatus	Periodical system

A good example of a film based on the concepts of the galaxy, human anatomy and proteins can be found here: www.youtube.com/watch?v=laDWBT8mgSw
(this film is in Dutch and was made by four first-year Beta-gamma students: Maarten van der Sande, Maria Stuut, Patrick Vlaar & Vikki de Jong).
The following list of concepts can be used if this learning activity is related to social-science-based courses:

Sociology	Economy	Political science
Functionalism	Barter economy	Nationalism
Civilization theory	Theory of comparative advantage	Clash of civilizations
Social cohesion	Theory of the invisible hand	Liberalism
Tragedy of the commons	Scarcity	Good governance/rule of law

Variations

If your students are not accustomed to connecting different disciplinary concepts, you could include a feedback moment on the script. Giving feedback will ensure that the end product is of a minimum quality.

If your students are familiar with connecting different disciplinary concepts you could make the assignment more difficult by including extra concepts from a fourth discipline.

The clips can be shown to a broader audience to finalize a course.

For an extra stimulus 'Oscars' could be awarded to the three best clips.

References

The framework of this ILA is derived from the curricular design within the Institute for Interdisciplinary Studies.

30 Panel discussion

Overview

Students learn to understand the different knowledge frameworks and evaluate the differences in approach of two disciplinary researchers by interviewing the researchers with the same set of questions aimed to elucidating the views of the researchers on a common topic.

Interdisciplinary skills	Reflection, dealing with cognitive biases, evaluating		
Characteristics	workshop	course	curriculum
	individual	group	
Duration – activity	90 minutes		
Intended learning outcome	Students are able to formulate questions that gain a better understanding of a researcher's knowledge framework; Students are able to explain the similarities and differences in knowledge frameworks of disciplinary researchers.		
Remarks	This activity involves two researchers from different disciplinary backgrounds.		

Setup

a Preparation teacher

The teacher should organize a panel discussion with two open-minded researchers from different disciplinary backgrounds. It is important that you categorize and select the questions that the students will use in the interview ahead of the panel discussion to guarantee the quality of the panel discussion.

Tip: Look for researchers who are willing to get out of their comfort zone. They may be hidden in departments or based outside the college or university. The combination of educational and research background, personal interest and experiences make them suitable for this kind of endeavour.

b   Preparation student
The students have to hand in three questions that can be asked to the researchers.

c   Teaching setup
Step 1
Lecture before the panel discussion: Introduce the assignment at least one week before the panel discussion is planned. Explain that the students are going to interview two researchers from different disciplinary backgrounds about the same topic in the upcoming lecture. The students have to develop a set of questions on this topic to gain more insight into how the researchers approach the particular topic. The questions should be provoking and yet general enough that the researchers can both formulate an answer. This set of questions will be asked to the two researchers. After you explained the assignment briefly introduce the topic at stake and inform the students about the disciplinary background of each researcher.
Instruct the students to come up with three questions and have them hand them in. You can cluster the questions and make a selection of the questions that will be used in the panel discussion.

Step 2
At the start of the panel discussion lecture, assign a small group of students the role of 'scribes'. The scribes are responsible for making notes on how the researchers interpret the questions and what kind of information they provide. Before the first interview begins, have the researchers introduce themselves.
All the students are interviewers (except for the scribes) and are all assigned to ask one question. During twenty minutes students should be asking the first researcher the series of questions. Then the second researcher will be interviewed for twenty minutes with the same set of questions.

Step 3
After a short break, invite the two researchers to start a discussion that is led by the students. The goal of this discussion is to explore the complementary (non-conflicting) elements of knowledge derived from the disciplinary fields as well as the conflicting elements between both knowledge frameworks.
The group of students that acted as scribes provide the main input for this discussion, but all students can participate. Instruct the students that the starting point of the discussion should be the extent to which the two researchers interpreted the set of questions differently as a result of their different disciplinary backgrounds.

Example

Panel discussion on energy
In a course that involves exploring current issues on sustainability, a broad topic like 'energy' can be addressed in several ways.

The following two types of researchers could be chosen to participate in the interview and subsequent panel discussion prepared by the students:

- A researcher with a background in political science, specializing in the geopolitics of natural resources.
- A researcher with a background in chemistry, specializing in sustainable energy technologies.

Questions that students may come up with:

- Do you consider energy a scarce resource? If so, who or what makes it a scarce resource?
- Do you consider the quantity of energy available for human use a current problem? If so, what are the possible and viable solutions to that problem?
- What characteristics of energy determine our relationship to it?
- What are the most challenging developments in your field with regard to the energy problem?
- What are the most promising methodologies for research on the energy problem?

The goal of this discussion is to explore the complementary (non-conflicting) elements of knowledge derived from the disciplinary fields as well as the conflicting elements between both knowledge frameworks.

Variations

You could include a written reflection assignment in which the students give a summary of the knowledge frameworks of the two researchers and reflect on the complementary and conflicting elements. To make it more challenging you could ask the students to create common ground between the knowledge frameworks.

You can make the assignment more challenging by letting the students select the set of questions based on the questions they generated as a group.

To make it easier for the students to stimulate the panel discussion, you could decide to not have the second researcher present while the first one is answering the questions, or vice versa, so that one of the researchers does not know how the other researcher has dealt with the questions.

You can extend the duration of this activity by organizing several panel discussions on similar or other topics during the course, depending on the availability of the researchers.

References

The framework of this ILA is derived from the curricular design within the Institute for Interdisciplinary Studies.

31 OEPS model

Overview

The OEPS model helps students to give each other feedback without judgement. When preparing a group assignment, for example a research project, it is important to know how to provide constructive feedback to the other team members. This learning activity is suitable for one workshop, but you can also stimulate students to have several 'feedback' moments during the course, in order to stimulate a positive group atmosphere that will contribute to their teamwork outcomes.

Interdisciplinary skills	Reflection, shared leadership, evaluating		
Characteristics	workshop	course	curriculum
	individual	group	
Duration – activity	45 minutes		
Intended learning outcome	Students are able to give each other constructive feedback using the OEPS-model		
Remarks			

Setup

a   Preparation teacher

Prepare at least one case the students could practise with during the tutorial. In addition, one good and bad example of providing feedback could help students to see differences between the OEPS model, and the most common ways of providing feedback.

b   Teaching setup

Step 1

Divide the class into groups of 3-4 students.

Introduce the model visually.

- Observation: I have seen/noticed this.
- Effects: This is the effect it has on me.
- Pause: Give the other person the opportunity to react.
- Suggestion: How can the other person improve?

Explain the different steps. The OEPS model provides a method for feedback based on observable behaviour and not personality traits. To illustrate the OEPS model, give an example yourself. It could help to give one 'bad example' of providing feedback without the OEPS model, and then one 'good' example following the steps of the model.

Step 3
Show your prepared case(s) to the students. Discuss the case together. Analyse the issues between the different actors. It is important to create awareness for the fact that every person experiences situations differently. Next, discuss their motives and desires.

Step 4
Let the students practise as follows: Two students practise the conversation, while the third student observes and eventually gives his or her feedback. Monitor the atmosphere while walking around. It is important students take this exercise seriously, and really try to empathize with the people in the case(s) and follow the steps in the OEPS model.

Step 5
If you use more cases, introduce a new case and let the students change their roles.

Example
Below, three cases are described. These cases could be the starting point for step 4.

Case 1
A group of interdisciplinary students have to make a film about how elderly care in the Netherlands should be organized. Their backgrounds are economics, history and biology. During the project, the focus shifts towards a more economic perspective. The other two students are disappointed and want to quit the project. They have another two weeks before the deadline.

Case 2
Two students have to write a paper together. The first student is responsible for all the calculations and the second student is responsible for writing the paper. However, the second student's writing skills are not good and he is not willing to improve himself. The deadline approaches.

Case 3

A student has handed in an individual writing assignment. At the halfway stage, the student did not receive much feedback, apart from 'being right on track'. His final mark turned out to be a 6.3. The student is disappointed, as he could not find great differences between his papers and papers of other students. The teacher did not take the student's argumentation seriously. The bachelor coordinator forces the student to resolve his issues with the teacher himself.

Case 4

A student is late for class and walks into the classroom fifteen minutes after the class has started. This interrupts the teacher's lecture.

Example of feedback with the OEPS model (for Case 4, from teacher to student)
- Observation: I saw you coming into class fifteen minutes after the tutorial had started
- Effect: This affected me, as I got distracted and lost my storyline.
- Pause
- Suggestion: My suggestion is that, when you're late, you either check the window to see if you can enter the room without interrupting, or wait for the break.

Variations

Let students hand in their own cases (from their own experience in teamwork) before the start of the tutorial, and use these cases in step 4 (and 5).
If your course includes a group assignment, you can create a set of feedback moments during the course.

References

The framework of this ILA is derived from the curricular design within the Institute for Interdisciplinary Studies.

32 Developing a collaborative E-book

Overview

This learning activity can be combined with a series of lectures on different disciplinary perspectives on a topic. After students have written a disciplinary paper on a specific topic, they co-write a chapter on the same topic with students from different disciplines. In this chapter they have to integrate their various disciplinary insights into the topic. All the chapters together will be published in a collaborative E-book.

Interdisciplinary skills	Evaluating, reflection, formulating a common goal		
Characteristics	workshop	course	curriculum
	individual	group	
Duration – activity	90 minutes		
Intended learning outcome	Students are able to discuss their findings among peers and draw joint conclusions; Students are able to reflect on the work of peers and provide constructive feedback; Students are able to reflect on their own work and incorporate feedback from peers.		
Remarks			

Setup

a   Preparation teacher

This learning activity needs to be combined with a series of lectures around a topic that can be approached from different disciplinary perspectives, such as the social sciences, natural sciences and humanities.

b   Preparation student

c   Teaching setup
      Step 1 (week 1)
      During the first lecture introduce the topic and the core lecturers of the module.
      Make sure that you incorporate time so that the students get to know each other's
      disciplinary background and previous experiences with the topic. Also give an
      overview of the course and explain how the students are going to write a collaborative
      E-book during this module.

      Step 2 (week 2-3)
      In the second lecture, have students brainstorm is small groups about the topic.
      Instruct the small groups to involve the different disciplines (i.e. social sciences,
      natural sciences and humanities) in their brainstorm. Explain that two days before
      the third lecture each student has to hand in a preparatory assignment that includes
      a preliminary research question and what kind of subtopic they want to focus on.
      Stimulate students to choose a research question related to their own disciplinary
      background.

      Based on this preparatory assignment you form groups of 4-6 students with different
      disciplinary backgrounds that focus on the same subtopic (see also Finding a shared
      topic on page 86). This group will be responsible for a chapter of the collaborative
      E-book. At the end of the third lecture announce the group division and let students
      have their first group meeting.

      Tip: Recommend the groups to assign one or two persons in the group as a
      chairperson (main editor).

      Step 3 (week 4-8)
      Ask the students to write an individual paper on their chosen subtopic of
      approximately 3,200 words. In week eight the students hand in their first version.

      Tip: Remind the students a week before the deadline about the approaching deadline.

Step 4 (week 9-11)
      After the students hand in their individual paper organize a feedback session with
      their group members. Instruct students to read the individual papers written by their
      group members and provide feedback before that week's lecture. You provide the
      draft versions with feedback.
      At the end of the lecture invite the students to work on their book chapter as a group,
      by sharing their findings and exploring options for integration. The following two
      weeks (10-11) the students co-write their book chapter by merging their individual
      papers and writing a joined introduction and conclusion to their chapter.

Tip: Provide the students with a template for the structure and style (font type, referencing style, etc.) of the individual paper and book chapter by developing an editable document. By using a template, you overcome the differences in standards for academic publications in various disciplines.

Step 5

Organize a symposium where the groups present their book chapter. Each group has approximately 15-20 minutes for their presentation with room for questions and feedback afterwards. Two days after the symposium students submit their book chapter including the final versions of the individual paper. This way the students have time to incorporate the feedback based on their presentation to finalize their chapter.

Step 6

After the module, combine the book chapters in an E-book.

d   Assessment

Here are some examples of the assessment criteria for the book chapter that you can use to develop your own rubric. The individual papers are graded separately.

Abstract and introduction

- Does the abstract provide a concise summary of the main points of the book chapter?
- Is the introduction clear? (Aim of the chapter, relevance, central questions, etc.)
- Is a common framework created?

Integrated discussion and conclusion

- Do the authors provide an integrated analysis of the topic?
- Are the individual papers connected in an integrated discussion and conclusion?
- Do the authors reflect critically on insights from the individual papers and theory (lectures and literature)?
- What lessons can be learnt when bringing insights from the individual case studies together?

▼

Structure and style

- Structure of the paper (e.g. information presented in a logical way, structure clearly indicated, consistency of information).
- Academic writing style (grammar, spelling, readability, etc.).
- Reference list (correct, consistent).
- Layout as indicated in document 'layout for book chapter' and consistent.

The X factor

- Originality, creativity, curiosity, enthusiasm, out-of-the-box thinking.
- Visualizations (e.g. figures, tables, graphs etc.).
- Integration of insights from social sciences, natural sciences, humanities.

Example

During the elective module 'Islands: models for our planet, metaphors for our world' students co-wrote an interdisciplinary E-book about sustainability on different islands around the globe. Students choose an island and subtopic to focus on. The students that focused on the same island formed the group to write a chapter. This resulted in chapters on the Galapagos, the Falklands, Bonaire, Hawaii, the Maldives, Iceland and Madagascar.

These chapters covered a wide range of topics, including well-being, politics, culture, biodiversity, the economy, agriculture, tourism, energy, water, waste and climate. By writing a collaborative E-book students learn that many of these topics are intricately related when considering an island.

The collaborative E-book can be found at:
www.islandstudies.ca/sites/islandstudies.ca/files/MS%20374-5-ISLANDS%20 Models-for-our-Planet-Metaphors-for-our-World-eBook-2016.pdf

References

- Norder, S.J., & Rijsdijk, K.F. (2016). Connecting the social sciences, natural sciences and humanities. *Island Studies Journal*, 11(2), 673-686.

33 Instrumental sketchbook

Overview

This ILA trains students to use visual language to communicate about different perspectives on a particular topic. By using visual language, specialist vocabulary becomes to the point and understandable for students with a different disciplinary background. As a result, different perspectives become better transferable to other disciplinary contexts. Students learn how to interact between different disciplinary perspectives and their own perspective based on visual communication.

Interdisciplinary skills	Formulating a common goal, perspective taking, ordering & structuring		
Characteristics	workshop	course	curriculum
	individual	group	
Duration – activity	120 minutes per module		
Intended learning outcome	Students are able to reflect on their own way of thinking and the thinking of others regarding an issue or problem; Students have the ability to achieve team consensus about the solution to a problem; Students are able to order and structure thoughts concerning the problem in relevant categories.		
Remarks	You need the following material: sketchbooks, pencils, small (non-sticky) sheets of paper.		

Setup

a   Preparation teacher

Select one interdisciplinary problem for this learning activity that is related to your course. Prepare a couple of questions for the students so that they gain a better understanding of the problem Make sure that your questions cover six types of

questions – what, why, where, how, when/how many and who – to stimulate a variety
of perspectives and drawing types (see example below).
Prepare examples of visual vocabulary and of visual language related to the problem,
to explain the power of imagination and of open and nonlinear communication (after
step 2).
Provide a sketchbook and a pen per person and some stacks of small (non-sticky)
paper notes.

b   Preparation student
Students have to gain a better understanding of the chosen interdisciplinary problem
by reading literature that they search for themselves. This preparation will be the
basic input for the sketchbook.
Also instruct the students to create one image including a title of a possible solution
to that problem. The students can use their image as a start to communicate the
proposed solution in step 4 (see below).
Students continue practising their visual vocabulary by sketching pages of items
such as lines, metaphors, icons, diagrams, maps or timelines.

c   Teaching setup
Step 1: Stimulus (15 minutes)
Hand out a small sketchbook per student and a simple black pen. For this activity it
is important to activate the whole brain. You can do this by asking students to draw
themselves on the first page of their sketchbook and to add name, date and discipline
to the drawing. Then ask 'where are you right now?' and to draw the answer on the
following page and finally ask 'what attracts your attention when you look around?'
and to draw the answer.

Step 2: Show and share experiences (10 minutes)
Instruct the students to hold up their 'where' and 'what' sketches. Ask different
students to explain what they see on the sketch. Based on the students' answers you
can discuss the differences between intention and perception of the sketches in a
playful way. This will start making the students aware that they have to think about
how to visualize a core message.

Step 3: Reflecting and testing (40 minutes)
Divide the students in smaller groups of five students and provide the groups with
stacks of small (non-sticky) sheets of paper.
Firstly, ask students to draw at least five single and free thoughts about the
interdisciplinary problem (one thought per small sheet). When they finish drawing
their thoughts lay out all the small thought sheets per group. Let the students discuss
their drawings of single thoughts by asking each other: 'What is the meaning of this
drawing?' In this way students become aware of the different perspectives on the
complex problem and whether the sketch communicates the intended message. To
put more focus on the thought sketches, ask the students to add a single word to
every sketch that entails the core message.

After this discussion ask every group to sort out the thoughts by grouping all the sketches in four or five categories (for the categorization the students can use the words that entail the core messages of the sketches). Explain that after sorting the sketches the group has to decide on names per category of thought sketches and a title for the collection of all their thoughts.

Now arrange all sketches per group together in radial lines, around the sketch with the title in the middle. By *mapping* single thoughts this way every group member will have an overview of the different perspectives on the complex problem.

Next, ask every student to draw their personal interpretation of the group map of thoughts on a double page in the sketchbook. Let the students discuss their drawings. In this way students become aware that the categorization of thoughts related to the complex problems can be interpreted in various ways.

Lastly you make a final map as a visual conclusion of all group maps (on blackboard or flip chart) based on the visual input of all the students. This visualization will show the various perspectives on the complex problem.

Make sure that all produced thought sketches sheets will be collected in a *treasure box*. This treasure box resembles the common source of interdisciplinary reflection and students can use this for a future sketchbook exercise or visual communication input.

Step 4: Show and share an idea (30 minutes)

Instruct the group to mix up all the loose thought sketches and to spread them out to have an overview again. Explain that a storyline has a beginning, a middle and an end. Instruct the students to write down the solution to the complex problem in one sentence and add a title. They could use their homework assignment for inspiration for a proposed solution. Arrange the thought sketches in one long (curved) storyline with a beginning and an end that visualizes their proposed solution. Students can decide to put non-relevant sketches in the treasure box *again* and maybe add a few extra sketches to complete their story.

Next, ask the students to draw a story consisting of five pictures that explain the solution in their sketchbook based on their storyline.

After they finish with their stories, each group presents their story in front of all the students by showing the five sketches.

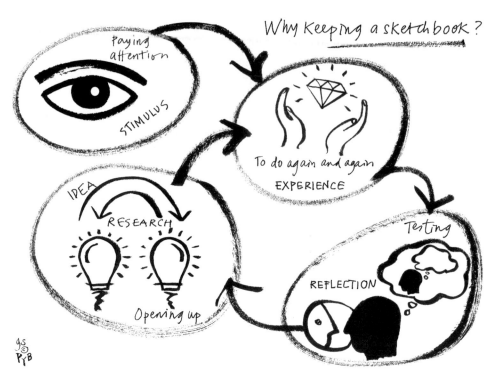

Why keeping a sketchbook?

Paying attention

STIMULUS

To do again and again
EXPERIENCE

IDEA
RESEARCH

Opening up

Testing

REFLECTION

d   Assessment

You could grade the students for their visual thinking and visual communication skills as practised in the final sketchbook. You could choose to grade a person or to grade a group by also taking the *treasure box* and the group production into account.

For example:
The skill of using functional drawing (20%)
- Are sketches clear and to the point?
- Are sketches relevant to thought?
- Do sketches attract the attention of others?

The quality of visual thinking (30%)
- Do drawings (structured sketches) provide critical insight of thought or idea?
- Do drawings (structured sketches) provide overview of a way of thinking?

The quality of visual communication (30%)
- Do sketches and drawing stimulate participation of fellow students or others?
- Do sketches and drawing open up misunderstanding within student groups or teams?

Instrumental use of the sketchbook (20%)
- Does the sketchbook contribute to the analysis of the problem?
- Does the sketchbook show typical interdisciplinary thinking?
- Does the sketchbook expose a structure of ideas?

Example

Public services

Public service is a topic studied in various academic fields, such as politics and economics. *How to empower public services?* could serve as an example of an interdisciplinary problem to be solved.

The following questions were used to prepare the students for this activity: What is a public service? Where do public services make a difference? Why is a service public? How is the public being served? Who is the public? When is a service public?

Variations

You could add an extra reflection step by letting the students compare their individual solution to the problem in their homework assignment with the storyline in step 4. In this way students can reflect upon how other perspectives influence the solution.

You could make a module of this activity by doing this activity multiple times with different topics to make students aware of different perspectives on a topic and how they are communicated in an effective way.

As an additional activity students could practise to prepare a visual presentation, for example an infographic (clever and clear), poster presentation (simple and short) or a slideshow (alert and attractive) by using a sketchbook to be instrumental for visual thinking and visual communication.

You could use this ILA during an interdisciplinary research project. With this activity project teams communicate in a more understandable way about their disciplinary contribution to the project. This could help students to find ways to integrate their disciplinary perspectives.

References

Drawing as a way of thinking developed from several MSc courses taught at the TU-Delft, from master classes for schools and institutions, such as Rijkswaterstaat, and from contributions to international conferences, such as IIS NIOC at University of Amsterdam.

Lesson modules are based on the method of *Name It Frame It Map It Show it* © by Germaine Sanders PICTURE YOUR BUSINESS® research advice and training For more information, see www.pyb-rotterdam.com (Dutch).

34 Writing a reflection essay

Overview

Reflecting on your own learning can make explicit one's preferred style of reasoning, analysing and evaluating. Moreover, it can be a way to bring to light cognitive biases. In this learning activity students learn to reflect on their own learning process during a specific course. In addition, they reflect on the development of their own interdisciplinary skills.

Interdisciplinary skills	Reflection, situation awareness, a questioning attitude		
Characteristics	workshop	course	curriculum
	individual	group	
Duration – activity	Depends whether you choose to do this during a course or as a curriculum activity (one semester or one academic year).		
Intended learning outcome	Students are able to reflect on their own learning process in a reflection essay.		
Remarks			

Setup

a   Preparation teacher

Prepare a reflection assignment for the students. This reflection assignment focuses on writing an essay about their (interdisciplinary) learning process.

b   Teaching setup

Step 1

Explain the reflection essay at the beginning of the course. This learning activity is a process that consists of three activities for students during the course:

1   Make explicit what you expect from the course: What do you hope to gain?
    Where are you now, regarding interdisciplinary skills (see the introduction of this

handbook for examples), and where do you wish to be at the end of the course? When do you consider the course a success?

2 Take notes in a course journal, reflecting on your learning experiences. What skills did you develop? How did you develop these skills? Was it hard or easy to develop these skills – and why? In what other situations than the course can you apply these skills? What is still to be learned regarding these skills?

3 Write a final reflection essay, in which you return to your pre-reflection and use your journal notes to answer the question raised there.

Step 2

At the start of the course, ask students to record their 'naïve' thoughts about the course in a **pre-reflection**.

You could tell students the following: This first reflection contains your *naïve* thoughts about the topic of the course. Notice that the word 'naïve' is not used pejoratively here, just descriptively: these were your thoughts before you were exposed to the course content. This pre-reflection will be part of the material you can later use for looking back. It's a vital part, as you tend all too easily to forget your naïve thoughts.

Step 3

Explain that students regularly need to take notes in a **course journal** during the course to make sure that the learning is documented. You could tell students the following: preferably every week (but certainly fortnightly), write down what you experienced during course work, what you learned from what you did, and what new insights you gained. Most often the insights will come only later, so don't despair if you feel you didn't have any early on in the course. Please also note your emotional response: Did you really like something, or hate something? Feelings are part of the process so don't ignore them.

Step 4

The students have to reflect upon what they learned during the course, especially in the most profound meaning in the **final reflection** essay.

You could tell them the following: As a starting point use your first reflection. Then use your course journal to help you reflect on your own naïve thoughts in the first reflection. Take the first reflection as raw material and reshape it, reflect upon it, rework it, all in the light of your course journal. Ask yourself:

■ What did I get from the course? What, how, when, and why did I learn?
■ What products, outcomes do I have to demonstrate this learning?
■ Did I just learn new facts or skills, or did this learning also provide me with new insights?
■ Which of the insights I gained do I value most?
■ What plans do I have to continue learning? What trained skills do I wish to develop further?

Finally, tell the students to write the essay in such a manner that any knowledgeable person could read and understand it. This also means weaving all the necessary background information into the essay.

Assessment(s)

You could use the following grading rubric and grading matrix. Be aware that literature on the effectiveness of assessing reflection in higher education shows that assessing reflection can easily inhibit proper reflection in students. Therefore, it is recommended to thoroughly think about the usefulness of assessing reflection before administering it and use it sparingly.

Grading rubric

	Poor (<50%)	Satisfactory (60-70%)	Good (70-85%)	Excellent (85-100%)
Pre-reflection	The pre-reflection is missing or doesn't address naïve thoughts of the student about ecology.	The pre-reflection addresses the naïve thoughts of the student about ecology. However, the pre-reflection is poorly structured.	The pre-reflection addresses the naïve thoughts of the student about ecology. Also, the pre-reflection is well structured. However, the presentation of the thoughts has no natural flow.	The pre-reflection addresses the naïve thoughts of the student about ecology. Also, the pre-reflection is well structured, and the presentation of the thoughts has a natural flow.
Journal notes				
Frequency	Fewer than five journal notes.	Between six and nine journal notes, not very extensive.	Between ten and twelve journal notes.	More than twelve journal notes.
Content	The notes are quite short and mostly summarizing class content.	The notes may be of appropriate length but hardly go beyond summarizing class content.	The notes are informative and clearly relate to course content. They do address more than just content, also how the content affected the student.	The notes are informative and clearly relate to course content as well as to how the student experienced the course material. Moreover, the student reflects on experiences outside the course context.

Reflection				
Structure of essay	The essay has a poor structure, there is no clear flow of information.	The essay has a reasonable overall structure, but some information is in the wrong place.	The essay has a good overall structure, but some information is in the wrong place.	The essay has an excellent overall structure and there is a strongly felt natural flow of information.
Connection to pre-reflection	There is little or no connection to the pre-reflection.	The pre-reflection is mentioned but content-wise there is little connection between the pre- reflection and the reflection.	The pre-reflection is clearly connected to the reflection, but the connection is not well balanced. Some aspects of the pre-reflection are more or less neglected.	The pre-reflection is clearly connected to the reflection, in a well-balanced way. All thoughts of the pre-reflection are addressed in the reflection.
Connection to course content	The reflection is poorly connected to course content. The connection is made explicit with only two or fewer examples.	The reflection is reasonably connected to course content. The connection is made explicit with at least three examples. The connection is addressed in a rather shallow way.	The reflection is well connected to course content. The connection is made explicit with four or five examples. The connection is addressed and explored in sufficient depth.	The reflection is well connected to course content. The connection is made explicit with at least five examples. The connection is addressed in a compelling way.
Use of journal notes	Journal notes are hardly used.	Journal notes are sparingly used, in a superficial way.	Journal notes are well used, but in a somewhat shallow way.	Journal notes are extensively used. Their relevance for the student's experience is explored in depth.

▼

Writing style				
Paragraphs	Paragraphs are either lacking or only typographical in nature. The one topic per paragraph-rule is violated on many occasions.	The one topic per paragraph-rule is more or less adhered to. Paragraph structure is under-developed.	The one topic per paragraph-rule is mostly well adhered to. Paragraph structure is quite developed and paragraphs do have an internal consistency.	The one topic per paragraph-rule is perfectly adhered to. Paragraph structure is well developed and paragraphs do have compelling internal consistency.
Sentence connection	Sentences are poorly if at all connected in most of the writing.	Sentence connection is regularly paid attention to but still quite often poorly structured.	Most sentences are well connected but occasionally there are clear gaps between the sentences, leading to hick-ups in the reading.	Sentences are perfectly connected and the reader never experiences hiccups in the reading.
Reference words	Reference words mostly have empty referents or refer to nouns too far back in the text to be unambiguous. Reference words are used to refer across paragraphs.	Reference words occasionally have empty referents or refer to nouns too far back in the text to be unambiguous.	The one topic per paragraph-rule is mostly well adhered to. Paragraph structure is quite developed and paragraphs do have an internal consistency.	The one topic per paragraph-rule is perfectly adhered to. Paragraph structure is well developed and paragraphs do have compelling internal consistency.
Spelling and grammar	Many mistakes in spelling and grammar.	Occasionally, there are mistakes in the spelling and grammar.	There are only afew mistakes in spelling and grammar.	The spelling and grammar are impeccable.

Layout and typography				
Title page	Title page is lacking or grossly incomplete.	Title page is present but some required information is lacking.	Title page presents all required information.	Title page presents all required information in a graphically appealing way.
Layout	Typography distracts from reading the document. The typography may be inconsistent (e.g. different font types in similar elements). Typography does not adhere to guidelines.	Typography is mostly consistent but does little to guide reading the report.	Typography is consistent and provides guidance is reading the document.	Typography is consistent and provides optimal guidance is reading the document
Typography does not fully adhere to guidelines.	Typography is consistent and provides guidance is reading the document.	Typography is consistent and provides optimal guidance is reading the document.	The one topic per paragraph-rule is mostly well adhered to. Paragraph structure is quite developed and paragraphs do have an internal consistency.	The one topic per paragraph-rule is perfectly adhered to. Paragraph structure is well developed and paragraphs do have compelling internal consistency.

	weight	grade 0 40 50 60 70 80 90 100	contribution to final grade
Pre-reflection	**20%**		
Journal notes	**20%**		
frequency			
content			
Reflection	**30%**		
structure			
connection to pre-reflection			
connection to course content			
use of journal notes			
Writing style	**20%**		
paragraphs			
sentence connection			
reference words			
spelling & grammar			
Layout & typography	**10%**		
title page			
layout			
Final grade	**100%**		

For the overarching criteria in colour you receive a partial grade; column B indicates the weight of the partial grade.

The criteria are broken down to various contributing aspects; with an 'x' I indicate where you roughly are on aspects. All these aspects together lead to the partial grade for the pertinent criterion, but not necessarily as the average.

Variations

A completed reflection assignment can be a useful tool to use during a personal conversation between you and the student.

References

The framework of this ILA is derived from the curricular design within Amsterdam University College.

Curricula

35 Reflection on (inter)disciplinarity

Overview

The students learn to reflect on the strengths and limitations of disciplinary perspectives and methodologies. In addition, they reflect on the development of their own interdisciplinary skills in a specific course or curriculum.

Interdisciplinary skills	Reflection, a questioning attitude, analysing		
Characteristics	workshop	course	curriculum
	individual	group	
Duration - activity	90 minutes		
Intended learning outcome	Depends whether you choose to do this during a course or as a curriculum activity (one semester or one academic year).		
Remarks			

Setup

a   Preparation teacher

Prepare a reflection assignment for the students. This reflection assignment focuses on their interdisciplinary learning process. There are several possible types of reflection assignments, such as:

- A reflection form with preformulated questions;
- Organizing reflection meetings between students and teachers;
- Encouraging students to prepare a discussion about their own interdisciplinary learning experience.

b   Teaching setup

Step 1 (beginning of the course)

Introduce the reflection assignment at the start of a course that has an explicit interdisciplinary focus. Explain the main goal of the assignment: Students have to reflect on their disciplinary and interdisciplinary learning processes. Depending on the type of reflection assignment, you have to either provide the students with a deadline (reflection form, reflection essay) or with dates for discussion(s) or meeting(s).

Step 2 (halfway in the course)

If a reflection form, a reflection essay or a reflective discussion is the final assignment in this course, one can address the assignment halfway in the course by discussing the following questions with the students:

- What do you think of your interdisciplinary learning thus far in the course?
- What skills have you developed to reflect on the pros and cons of the disciplines covered in the course?
- To what extent have your initial ideas on the utility and value of interdisciplinary research changed during this course?

For reflection meetings it is important to plan at least one meeting halfway in the course. The questions presented above can be discussed with the students during this meeting.

Tip: Make sure you write down the most noteworthy reflective comments that are made during this discussion, as these could be useful for future adjustments to the course.

Step 3 (end of the course)

For the reflection essay: Schedule time for a final reflection on the same questions that were mentioned in the previous step. It is advised to do this in the seminar before the students are due to hand in their completed reflection assignment.

c   Assessment

You can use a reflection form (i.e. the reflective questionnaire presented below) or a reflective essay as an assignment.

Example

A reflective questionnaire

Assignment: Reflection on interdisciplinarity

Since interdisciplinarity is also an attitude, we believe it is helpful for you to reflect on your development in the process of becoming interdisciplinary academics. To activate this reflection mode, a reflection form that addresses your own interdisciplinary learning has been developed.

Assignment instructions

Answer the following questions three times: once at the beginning of the course, once halfway through the course and once at the end of this course. You should also reflect on your previous answers, as this will help you to track how your thoughts about your own interdisciplinary learning may have changed over time.

Reflection on personal characteristics

1 According to you, what characteristics (interests, knowledge, skills, personal characteristics, etc.) does one need in order to succeed as an interdisciplinary academic?

2 Which of these characteristics do you already possess, and which do you need to acquire or develop?

3 Can you describe where you are in the process of 'becoming an interdisciplinarian'? Please describe the difficulties you have encountered and the successes you have had thus far. What would you like to change in your learning process?

Reflection on content

4 Which disciplines and/or subjects do you find the most interesting? Do certain disciplines dominate your interests? Please explain why (not).

5 How do your preferences for specific disciplines affect your perception of the advantages and shortcomings of interdisciplinary research and your own interdisciplinary learning process?

6 What insights do you have regarding combining and integrating several disciplinary insights, and when this is useful and when it is not?

Variations

One can vary the assignment in different courses, based on the disciplinary and interdisciplinary experience and knowledge of the students. If a bachelor or master programme has an interdisciplinary focus, the assignment could be expanded over two or three years, the same assignment can be handed out every year in order to follow the students (inter)disciplinary development.

Divide the students into groups of three at the start of the last seminar. The students hand their portfolio to the others. They then ask each other questions about their interdisciplinary development.

Furthermore, a completed reflection assignment can be a useful tool to use during a personal conversation between you and the student.

Grading: If you use a grading system for this assignment, ask the students to recall some of the previous conclusions (recorded in the halfway questionnaire) and verify to what extent these thoughts still hold.

References

The framework of this ILA is derived from the curricular design within the Institute for Interdisciplinary Studies & Interdisciplinary Social Sciences.

36 Reflection from different perspectives

Overview

In order to improve synthesis in their student career, students are challenged to reflect from different perspectives on how courses, course elements, a curriculum or extracurricular activities have contributed to their development. Moreover, this learning activity makes explicit a student's development in disciplinary and interdisciplinary skills and attitudes.

Interdisciplinary skills	Reflection, perspective taking, evaluating		
Characteristics	workshop	course	curriculum
	individual	group	
Duration – activity	One academic year or a whole curriculum.		
Intended learning outcome	Students are able to describe their development in different professional and personal roles; Students are able to relate their level of development in their roles to the required level at the end of the programme.		
Remarks	Assessment is often done by way of a portfolio; a formative assessment of (yearly) reflections helps students write a final reflection for the summative assessment at the end of their studies.		

Setup

a   Preparation teacher

Prepare a reflection assignment for the students. As this reflection assignment focuses on the reflection on students' development from different perspectives, you have to describe different roles that are important for your students. You may find inspiration for these roles in the intended programme outcomes; you can categorize different end terms under each role. For example, the programme outcomes 'the student has interdisciplinary research skills' and 'the student has experienced the methods of researchers in the chosen specialization', could correspond to the role of 'researcher'.

Once you have identified the different roles, you have to formulate different questions that help students reflect from different perspectives. In their role as researcher, for example, first-year bachelor students could be asked whether they have noticed how different disciplines have different requirements regarding scientific papers. Stress that in answering these questions it is not just important for a student to note that s/he has learned something, but also *what* s/he has learned and *how* s/he has learned this.

b   Preparation student
None.

c   Teaching setup
Step 1 (beginning)
Introduce the reflection assignment at the start of course, an academic year or a programme. Explain the main goals of the assignment: Students learn to connect learning experiences and learn to reflect on how their learning experiences contribute to their personal and academic development. Provide the students with the assignment (including a deadline).

Step 2 (halfway)
Remind students to make notes during and after courses on their learning experiences. This will help them with writing their evaluation at the end of the course/ year/ programme.

Step 3 (end)
Students have to hand in their completed reflection assignment.

d   Assessment
You can use the reflective essay as an assignment (see the grading rubric in the example below).

Example

At the bachelor Liberal Arts and Sciences at Utrecht University, students are asked to write a reflection assignment of 1,500 words at the end of their first semester and at the end of each academic year. Students are asked to reflect on five different roles, which are described as follows:

1   The researcher: Someone who knows how to formulate relevant research questions, answers these questions in a scientifically responsible way, and is able to present his or her findings in an adequate manner to a relevant forum.

2   The specialist: Someone who has obtained knowledge, insights and skills in one discipline. This means, among other things, that this person can evaluate both his/her own work and that of others adequately, responding to the criteria that are

common in that scientific discipline.

3   The intellectual: Someone who has obtained a good level of general and cultural development and has a broad perspective that crosses the borders of his or her own discipline. An intellectual is able to adequately connect insights from different scientific disciplines.

4   The professional: Someone who takes responsibility for his or her own performance and development. This means that a professional systematically analyses his or her own behaviour and uses this to set adequate goals and make adequate decisions.

5   The citizen: Someone who has a clear take on what to do outside academia and professional life. A responsible citizen reflects on his or her place in society (now and in the future).

Students are asked to reflect on these different roles at the end of their first semester and at the end of every academic year. At the end of the first year, the assignment is as follows:

1   As a researcher: After your first year you have gained experience in writing papers (formal writing assignments, in which you were asked to meet the scientific criteria). Describe what you think is most important in a scientific paper. Did you notice whether there are different criteria for papers in various disciplines? Do not just describe that you have learned something, but clearly state what you have learned and how you learned this. Evaluate your proceedings and add documents that support this – for example, papers.

2   As a (future) specialist: You have chosen a major. How did you make this decision and what do you expect to learn from your major?

3   As an intellectual: Describe – or better explain – how the interdisciplinary courses have contributed to your development as an interdisciplinary thinker. Try to explain how each course contributes to the bigger picture and aim for as few 'loose ends' (courses that are not placed in this bigger whole) as possible.

4   As a professional: In the end terms of the bachelor Liberal Arts and Sciences the professional attitude is described as 'being able to plan a project and to execute this plan, is able to work in a team and has the necessary social and communicative skills'. To what extent have the interdisciplinary courses contributed to your development of these skills? (Reminder: Describing is good, explaining is better). Did you develop your collaboration skills in other courses too?

5   The citizen: Students and alumni of the bachelor Liberal Arts and Sciences often think about complex societal problems such as sustainability or justice. Is there a specific cause you are committed to? Have you started wondering what you might want to contribute outside academia and professional life?

Role	Criterion	Describing (what?)	Explaining (how?)
1. Researcher	Evaluates his/her own proceedings regarding research skills.		
2 Intellectual	Is aware of the ways of thinking in the different disciplinary courses.		
	Compares and contrasts research fields and methods.		
	Seeks and discovers/creates substantive relationships between the different courses.		
	Describes/explains how knowledge from one discipline can be applied in another context.		
3. Specialist	Provides argumentation for decisions in the academic career.		
4. Professional	Provides a personal development analysis (content, personal, and/or contextual).		
	Describes/explains how extracurricular activities influence his or her personal development.		
5. Citizen	Reflects on his or her place in society (now and in the future).		

Variations

Have students draw a line with on the left 'start' and on the right the intended learning outcome (i.e. specialist). Have them reflect on where they stand on this line. To what extent have they progressed on the line (towards the intended learning outcome)? What do they still have to learn to reach the learning outcome (i.e. what do they have to learn to become a specialist)?

References

The framework of this ILA is derived from the bachelor Liberal Arts and Sciences at Utrecht University.

References

Association of American Colleges. (2007). *College learning for the new global century: A report from the National Leadership Council for Liberal Education & America's Promise.* Association of American Colleges.

Boix Mansilla, V., Dawes Duraisingh, E., Wolfe, C.R., & Haynes, C. (2009). Targeted Assessment Rubric: An Empirically Grounded Rubric for Interdisciplinary Writing, *The Journal of Higher Education,* 80(3), 334-353.

Cannon-Bowers, J.A., & Salas, E. (1997). A framework for developing team performance measures in training. In M.T. Brannick, E. Salas, & C. Prince (Eds.), *Series in applied psychology. Team performance assessment and measurement: Theory, methods, and applications* (pp. 45-62). Mahwah, NJ: Lawrence Erlbaum Associates.

De Greef, L., Post, G., Vink, C., & Wenting, L. (2017). *Designing interdisciplinary education: A practical handbook for university teachers.* Amsterdam: Amsterdam University Press.

Facione, P. (2011). *Measured Reasons and Critical Thinking.*

Ivanitskaya, L., Clark, D., Montgomery, G., & Primeau, R. (2002). Interdisciplinary learning: Process and outcomes. *Innovative Higher Education,* 27(2), 95111.

Manathunga, C., Lant, P., & Mellick, G. (2006). Imagining an interdisciplinary doctoral pedagogy. *Teaching in Higher Education,* 11(3), 365379.

Menken, S., & Keestra, M. (2016). *An Introduction to Interdisciplinary Research: Theory and Practice.* Amsterdam: Amsterdam University Press.

National Academy of Sciences (2005). *Facilitating interdisciplinary research.* Washington: The National Academies Press.

Newell, W.H. (1990). Interdisciplinary curriculum development. *Issues in Integrative Studies,* 8(1), 6986.

Newell, W.H. (2007). Decision making in interdisciplinary studies. *Public administration and Public Policy New York,* 123, 245.

Nosich, G.M. (2012). *Learning to think things through: A guide to critical thinking across the curriculum.* Boston: Pearson.

Paul, R., & Elder, L. (2009). *The miniature guide to critical thinking: Concepts and tools (6th ed.).* Dillon Beach, CA: Foundation for Critical Thinking.

Repko, A.F. (2008). Assessing interdisciplinary learning outcomes. *Academic exchange quarterly,* 12(3), 171.

Repko, A.F., Szostak, R., & Buchberger, M.P. (2013). *Introduction to interdisciplinary studies.* Thousand Oaks, CA: Sage Publications.

Spelt, E.J., Biemans, H.J., Tobi, H., Luning, P.A., & Mulder, M. (2009). Teaching and learning in interdisciplinary higher education: A systematic review. *Educational Psychology Review,* 21(4), 365378.

Terenzini, P.T., & Pascarella, E.T. (1991). Twenty years of research on college students: Lessons for future research. *Research in Higher Education,* 32(1), 8392.

Vogt, J., & Roblin, N.P. (2012). A comparative analysis of international frameworks for 21st-century competences: Implications for national curriculum policies. *Journal of Curriculum Studies,* 44(3), 299321.

Appendix

Boix Mansilla, V., Dawes Duraisingh, E., Wolfe, C.R., & Haynes, C. (2009). Targeted Assessment Rubric: An Empirically Grounded Rubric for Interdisciplinary Writing, *The Journal of Higher Education*, 80(3), 334-353.

Targeted Assessment Rubric for Interdisciplinary Writing

Category 1: Purposefulness				
Guiding question	Naïve	Novice	Apprentice	Master
1.1. Does the student's framing of the problem invite an integrative approach?	The paper does not contain an identifiable purpose or the purpose is unclear.	The paper contains a discernible purpose but it is not clear that this purpose calls for an integrative approach. *Or* The student does identify a problem that calls for an integrative approach but the purpose of the paper is not clearly stated or the purpose is unviable.	The student clearly states a purpose that calls for an integrative approach. However, the student offers no clear rationale or justification for taking this approach. *Or* The purpose of the paper appears somewhat ambitious	The student clearly states a purpose that calls for an integrative approach and provides a clear rationale or justification for taking this approach.
1.2. Does the student use the writing genre effectively to communicate with his or her intended audience?	There is little sense of an academic genre being used and the intended audience is unclear.	An academic genre is discernible but multiple violations of the genre (e.g. organization, tone, referencing, vocabulary) limit the student's ability to communicate with the intended audience. *Or* The writing is not fluid. It requires multiple readings.	An academic genre is clear and generally adhered to. The student is obviously aware of the intended audience, which often represents more than one discipline. The paper reads fluidly. No innovation within the genre is visible or if there is any attempt at innovation it is not effective. The paper may include minor errors in tone, mechanics and referencing.	An academic genre is clear and consistently adhered to. The student is obviously aware of the intended audience, which often represents more than one discipline. Any innovation within the genre is effective and deliberate.

Guiding question	Naïve	Novice	Apprentice	Master
2.1. Does the student use disciplinary knowledge accurately and effectively (e.g. concepts, theories, perspectives, findings, examples)?	A disciplinary knowledge base is not discernible in the sense that the ideas and information included do not stem from any particular disciplinary tradition. Misconceptions and folk beliefs abound. In some cases, jargon is used with little evidence of understanding. *And/or* the student misuses sources in a major way – e.g. non-credible sources, mis-understanding the meaning of source(s), relying too heavily on one source.	The student uses disciplinary concepts, theories, perspectives, findings, or examples in simplistic, general, or mechanical ways – as in the 'textbook' version of a discipline. Key claims are sometimes not supported, or concrete disciplinary examples are disconnected from key claims. Some misconceptions and unwarranted use of jargon may be present. Sources are used pro-forma.	Concepts and theories are used effectively in accordance to their disciplinary origins, in ways adopted by disciplinary experts. Theories and generalizations are consistently supported with examples or findings from the disciplines involved. Conversely, concrete cases and examples are interpreted with disciplinary concepts and theories. Relevant and credible sources are used intelligently to advance the argument of the piece, though the paper may have too many unnecessary sources, or key sources may be missing.	In addition to the qualities outlined at Level 3, a well-organized network of concepts, theories, perspectives, findings and examples within one or more of the selected disciplines is clearly visible. Some insightful new examples, interpretations, or responses within the selected disciplines may be present. There is sophisticated use of sources. The sources used are relevant and credible and integrated thoughtfully and purposefully to advance the student's argument.
2.2. Does the student use disciplinary methods accurately and effectively (e.g. experimental design, philosophical argumentation, textual analysis)?	The student shows little to no awareness of the methods, habits of mind and validation criteria by which knowledge is constructed and verified in the disciplines. Opinions and information summaries are presented as matters of fact.	The student shows awareness of or uses disciplinary methods and modes of thinking in one or more of the included disciplines, but employs them mechanically, superficially, or algorithmically. There may be oversimplifications and misconceptions about methods (e.g. if someone assumes statistics results are true).	The student accurately employs methods, modes of thinking (e.g. ways to select evidence or construct causal accounts), and validation criteria to construct knowledge in one or more of the selected disciplines.	The student accurately employs methods, habits of mind, and validation criteria to construct knowledge in one or more of the selected disciplines. He or she does so effectively, exhibiting language that describes the constructed nature of disciplinary knowledge (e.g. the provisional nature of insights, the limits of generalizations, the multiplicity of interpretations).

Category 3: Integration

Guiding question	Naïve	Novice	Apprentice	Master
3.1. Does the student include selected disciplinary perspectives or insights from two or more disciplinary traditions (presented in the course or from elsewhere) that are relevant to the purpose of the paper?	The paper shows no evidence that *disciplinary* perspectives are used to address the paper's purpose. Multiple perspectives or points of view may be considered but these do not represent *disciplinary* views and/or are not clearly related to the paper's purpose.	The paper includes two or more relevant disciplinary perspectives or fields but the connections between the included disciplinary insights and the purpose of the work are superficial or unclear. Crucial disciplinary perspectives may be missing.	The paper includes two or more relevant disciplines or fields. Selected disciplinary insights are clearly connected to the purpose of the work. Disciplinary perspectives that are tangential to the purpose may be present, or relevant perspectives missed.	The paper includes two or more relevant disciplines or fields. Selected disciplinary insights are clearly connected to the purpose of the work. No unrelated disciplinary insights appear and no crucial perspectives are missing. If the paper includes some tangential perspectives, which are, however, original it should be considered Level 4 for this criterion.
3.2. Is there an integrative device or strategy (e.g. a model, metaphor, analogy)?	The student may explore the topic in a holistic way but connections are unclear and there is no obvious sense of integration.	The student may explore the topic in a holistic way, making valid connections across disciplinary or field perspectives; however, insights from different perspectives are not integrated coherently or effectively. In some cases, disciplinary concepts, theories, perspectives, findings, or examples are placed side by side; connections and analogies are made but no overall coherent integration is discernible.	An integrative device (e.g. a leading metaphor, a complex causal explanation) clearly brings disciplinary insights together in a generally coherent and effective way.	A novel, imaginative, or well-articulated integrative device (e.g. a leading metaphor, a complex causal explanation) is used to bring disciplinary insights together in a coherent and effective way.

3.3. Is there a sense of balance in the overall composition of the piece with regard to how the student brings disciplinary perspectives or insights together to advance the purpose of the piece?	The paper shows an imbalance in the way particular disciplinary perspectives are presented in light of the purpose of the work (e.g. particular disciplinary perspectives are given disproportionate weight for no obvious reason).	The student attempts to balance perspectives but builds this on artificial or algorithmic grounds rather than substantive ones (e.g. giving equal weight to each disciplinary perspective studied irrespective of its substantive relevance to the problem at hand).	Disciplinary insights in the paper are generally balanced on substantive grounds in light of the purpose of the work. However, one or more aspects of the argument may be weakly addressed.	Disciplinary insights are delicately balanced to maximize the effectiveness of the paper in light of the purpose of the work. The integration is elegant and coherent and there are no distractions in the building of the argument.
3.4. Do the conclusions drawn by the student indicate that understanding has been advanced by the integration of disciplinary views?	The student attempts to make connections across different perspectives but these are unrelated to the apparent purpose of the paper.	Minor efforts at integration are present. Or a language of integration is present but is used mechanistically to yield minimal advancement toward the intended purpose.	The student makes a valid integration of disciplinary insights to generate understandings linked to the purpose of the paper. However, some obvious opportunities to advance the purpose of the paper are overlooked or undeveloped.	The student takes full advantage of the opportunities presented by the integration of disciplinary insights to advance his or her intended purpose both effectively and efficiently. The integration may result in novel or unexpected insights.

Category 4: Critical Awareness

Guiding question	Naïve	Novice	Apprentice	Master
4.1. Does the student show awareness of the limitations and benefits of the contributing disciplines or how the disciplines intertwine?	There is no awareness of the differing contributing disciplines or fields or their benefits or limitations (e.g. the topic is only approached from a common-sense or very general standpoint).	There is awareness of which disciplines are being used but there is no or only brief discussion of the limitations and/or benefits of the disciplinary contributions. There may be some misconceptions about how the disciplines are being used.	The benefits and/or limitations of the differing contributing disciplines or fields are sufficiently and clearly discussed. Some of the points made may be general or obvious.	The benefits and/or limitations of the differing contributing disciplines or fields are discussed clearly, insightfully, and in relationship to one another (e.g. students not only describe individual contributions but highlight how views complement, balance, add empirical grounding or put into question insights from other disciplines included in the work).
4.2. Does the student exhibit self-reflection?	The student does not consider the strengths and limitations of his or her own paper. Ideas are presented at face value without scepticism or reflection.	Comments on the strengths and limitations of the paper and its integrative approach seem mechanical, superficial, or in passing. Ideas are mostly presented at face value without scepticism or reflection.	There is sufficient comment on the strengths and / or limitations of the paper and its integrative approach, although the points made may be general or obvious.	There is consistent awareness of the strengths and limitations of the paper and its integrative approach. A tentative tone is adopted and alternative integrative approaches may be considered.

Colophon

About the authors

- Hannah Edelbroek lectures for the Bachelor's programme Natural and Social Sciences. She is specialized in cognitive neuropsychology and health care ethics.
- Myrte Mijnders lectures for the Bachelor's programme Natural and Social Sciences and the programme Future Planet Studies. She is specialized in evolution and sustainability.
- Ger Post lectures at the Bachelor's programme Natural and Social Sciences and the Master's programme Brain and Cognitive Sciences. He is the co-author of two handbooks for interdisciplinary students

About the University of Amsterdam

The University of Amsterdam (UvA) is one of the largest comprehensive universities in Europe, with some 30,000 students, 5,000 staff, and a budget of more than 600 million euros. The University provides academic training in all areas of science and scholarship and welcomes students and staff from all backgrounds, cultures and faiths who wish to devote their talents to the development and transfer of academic knowledge as a rich cultural resource and foundation for sustainable progress.

About the Institute for Interdisciplinary Studies

The Institute for Interdisciplinary Studies (IIS) is the University of Amsterdam's knowledge centre for interdisciplinary learning and teaching. It develops new courses in collaboration with the faculties.

The IIS has more than fifteen years experience in interdisciplinary education and continuously develops substantive education innovations with an interdisciplinary character. The Institute identifies new themes and issues linked to current developments in academia and society.

Over 3,000 students study at the IIS. The IIS offers a number of interdisciplinary study programmes along with a wide range of electives (minors, honours modules and various public events) for students from any faculty, for staff and for members of the public. All its activities are interdisciplinary in nature and are designed in collaboration with one or more faculties.

About the series
Interdisciplinary education and research is becoming increasingly popular in and outside academia. Yet there is still a demand for a theoretical and practical framework that describes what interdisciplinarity entails and how it can be realised in practice.

The *Perspectives on Interdisciplinarity* series is designed to address these needs and enable universities and curriculum leaders to shape interdisciplinary learning, teaching and research. The books in this series provide students, teachers and curriculum developers with insights into the broad field of interdisciplinary studies, offering practical tools for addressing the challenges that arise when taking an interdisciplinary approach.

The authors and editors who contributed to the publications are all engaged both conceptually and practically in interdisciplinary education and research.

The series welcomes monographs and edited volumes in English and Dutch by both established and early-career researchers, teachers or curriculum developers on topics such as student textbooks for interdisciplinary courses, educational approaches to enhance interdisciplinary understanding, methods for interdisciplinary research, and interdisciplinary theory and methodology.

Contact
Institute for Interdisciplinary Studies
Science Park 904
1098 XH Amsterdam
Tel. +31 20 525 51 90
www.iis.uva.nl
Onderwijslab-iis@uva.nl